SYLLABLE SOCCER

By
Anika Snyder

All rights reserved under International and
Pan-American copyright Conventions.
Published/Manufactured in the
United States of America.

Cover design by Mike Mulcahy
(**www.blackironcreative.com**)

Edited by Natalie June Reilly

No part of this publication may be reproduced or transmitted in any form or by any means, electronic or mechanical, including photocopy, recording or any information storage and retrieval system, without express written permission of the author.

Copyright © 2025 Anika Irene Snyder
All rights reserved.
ISBN: 979-8-998-5503-0-0

For Bob Garmston,
the literary light that led me to
my love of linguistic larks.

Table of Contents

Syllable Soccer   1

This section indulges my desire to mix up metaphor and manipulate meaning. Most of the poems were written intentionally for their melody; that specific music words make when mashed up against each other. If you have hiking boots, take the book on a walk for this portion. I am partial to the rhythm rhyme creates for walking.

Nature Break   65

The nature breaks are meant to provide a little respite from the heavy poems. They are an ode to the wonders of the natural world. My work has brought me ample opportunity for retrospective instruction, carried out by witnessing the delightful way the earth works. I find myself so frequently inspired by the simplicity of the outdoors and deeply indebted to the feeling of expansiveness it provides me.

We Named It Duress   75

I am gloomy. I am dull. I am a pessimistic person! This is where you find proof of that. Take care!

Nature Break   133

The nature breaks are meant to provide a little respite from the heavy poems ...

Men (Swearing, Power Steering, and Me)   145

I'm sorry, Mom. I'm sorry, Dad. I'm sorry, men who think me good when I've been bad! I'm the worst kind of romantic (nearly not at all), but here are poems to immortalize the fallen.

Nature Break — 229

The nature breaks are meant to provide a little respite from the heavy poems ...

Drinking (Oops! I Did It Again) — 241

Have you ever felt at the top of the world at the bottom of the bottle? The larger the lager, the later the emotional pain. It might be kicking the can down the road, but at least syllable soccer is sustained.

The Foxhole, The Atheist, Mathematic Conversion — 263

This is the section for the religiously cynical or searching. I've found myself lurching from belief to belief, like I'm walking on stars, drawing constellations of conclusions. If you take anything from this, make sure that they're all questions.

Nature Break — 279

The nature breaks are meant to provide a little respite from the heavy poems ...

Death (This Is All Just Conjecture) — 291

And taxes, more like. But the scythes are hooked around our middles, and I suppose my consideration of it is just really good prep work.

Hopeful Ending — 321

I am feeling magnanimous. Here is the hopeful ending I will provide for the damage done by the patently unhopeful work preceding it.

Syllable Soccer

This section indulges my desire to mix up metaphor and manipulate meaning. Most of the poems were written intentionally for their melody, that specific music words make when mashed up against each other. If you have hiking boots, take the book on a walk for this portion. I am partial to the rhythm rhyme creates for walking.

ANIKA SNYDER

SOUP

You and me.
We soup together—tomato bisque.
We spoon together.
We Caesar salad,
Omelet,
Cake ...
That's all the forking I can take.

AT CAPACITY

My youthfulness rests on an ivory fulcrum,
Whose foremost tip leaks noxious fumes
From a small silver crack.
Get back!
It hisses
At oceans,
At Space,
At any wide-open place
Where I can be fully myself.
My childhood shame
Can be tamed
In unconfined vastness.
So, I avoid it at all costs.

ANIKA SNYDER

GREEN

I am the green stalk growing through grates,
A fantastic image of industry intersecting
With natural order.
I am unreal and moldable,
Foldable
As a weak hand of cards,
Or the used duvet
You say
Still smells like her.

I am the ring light that forgets
The corners of the room
And assumes
Your face
Fills the space
Entirely!
I am the fire that we make plans for—
Because we know how fast I burn
And learn
To avoid hot-headed speech.

I am the peach
That you leave too long
In the throng of candy wrappers.
I am delayed release,
The sweet increased until I rot.

SYLLABLE SOCCER

JOIN IF YOU HAVE TO

Join if you have to.
Cults—your hands together.
Pharmacology.
Deuteronomy.
Join if you have to.

Leave—
The enterprise of singularity,
To beta fish and the sun.
Listen to the masses—
Art classes and half-filled glasses
At bar counters that stick to your fingers
And your credit cards.

Join if you have to.
Your voice to another—
Some choir council that forgets itself
In midnight adagios.
The slow.
Winding down.
Of conversation that leaves
The latent lull of loneliness
On red, sore tongues like film.

Join if you have to.
And leave me the hell out of it!
Like beta fish and the sun,
Let me run ahead
And hide.

T.O.M. (THINK OF ME)

Think of me when life is boring!
Like an obstreperous sea,
Or a watered-down hindsight—
Something you couldn't do justice to
With a few descriptive words.

Think of me when life is boring!
(And though I may alarm your amygdala,
Your poor lizard brain),
At least it is not dulling your day
To remember me.

Let me sharpen you.
My teeth come to a point.
Let me sheer you to the finest spear I can muster.

If you have fear,
If you are flustered,
I will not begrudge your egress
Because I know when life is lacking.
You'll return.

SYLLABLE SOCCER

BUT THEN AGAIN

I pull a lot of things:
Muscles,
Your leg,
My face at toddlers, behind their mothers' back.

My tendons are always sore
From my tender extrication of things—
Extrication being a fancy word for pulling.
(Indulge me.)

On the days when my tendons are tired,
I tend to retire by nightfall.
Cocooning myself in garish things,
Like the "forgiveness of others,"
Or the unforgiving glare of my phone.

I lead a ...
Very.
Little.
Life.

So, tiny things can be destructive!
Like unplanned for interruptions—
Or corruption of morals.

I have no quarrels with the world—
(Save my own insurrection.)
I keep trying to follow the rules
But that is one thing
I cannot pull
Off.

BRING ME YOUR TIRED & WEARY

Bring me your tired, weary, and fundamentally fucked up.
We will work it out together.
If I have news to parse through,
I'll let them have it first and watch their faces to see
which prescription I'll need to pop to hear it!

Bring me your tired, weary, and fundamentally fucked up.
If they need shelter, tell them, "Sorry, I only have room
for me and my bitch roommate sorrow."
If they get a little angry, tell them, "You can move in, and
I'll move out, but you'll acquire the bitch roommate
AND my doubt."

Bring me your tired, weary, and fundamentally fucked up.
I don't think it matters if they hate adorable things.
Like frayed strings ... or my own
uncommonly cute dissolution—
But let them not hate the thing as a whole.

(Garments, me)

Balloon, Picture Pin, Punctured Grin

My fantasies are fixtures I entertain
With unnerving sincerity.
My fictitious life is so much more
Rewarding than reality.
I concoct a different world
So that I can't feel life's disparity.
But all I've really done,
I fear,
Is make my life a parody.

Anika Snyder

WE NAMED IT DURESS

It grows in thin air,
On smooth minds.
The body,
A bend in loose spines—
The tomes are worn out tones
Our eyes cannot sing.
We named it duress.
It knows everything.

DOORMAT

I am a doormat!

I welcome you.

I am the cat's favorite thing to claw.

I am unlawful … but good!

Always around when you need me.

I am permitted a shape.

I cannot wait to unravel.

HOLLER

I showed up late to my own funeral.

Everyone had their eyes closed.

I suppose it was not a wake.

At Least I Can Face It

My torso is slowly disappearing.

I can feel the parts of me that reside there

Blink out like stars.

My liver leaves—

My heart,

My stomach.

My gallbladder has the gall to stick around.

I beg my core; I say, "Pray reconsider!"

My appendix bursts ...

Out laughing at my tears.

My uterus lines herself in handsewn linen.

She shrugs, "At least you have your lips and ears."

NET NEUTRALITY

I yearn   I want   I pine   I starve   I love the rot

   Of emptiness   When I fail   And fill me up

      I come undone   in rancidness

Syllable Soccer

FOUND POEM (THANKS, JACK!)

Humanity went to the moon and left me behind.
Now, it's me and my mind.
(I don't mind.)
I kind of like the way the emptiness makes me feel.
Immense.
I like the tense moment of regret,
When I forget to feed the children
And then remember they are crater caterers,
Mining moon stones for their mounting rock
Collections.
If I saw them again, I'd tell them to kick them—
The rocks that is.
Because the loneliness of the moment
Is so effortlessly divine ...
That I pine for nothing but a landline to the sky.

Sally & Shells, She Might Have Sold Some

And even though her shade is kind,
She loves the sun.
She often twines
Her fingers through the world's thick hair.
We lice can jump the hurdles there.

One leap beyond a karmic nail,
We falter and begin to fail.
In trestles of an endless dream,
I've found the rip.
She'll sew the seam.

Your Love For Me
Has Never Been Sincere

I am pepper.
I am penicillin.
I make you sneeze.
Wheeze.

I am the leaves that bleed poison—
Ivy that climbs trellises with tremulous fingers.
I am the medicinal high
That buys time for bigger minnows.

The pan—
Oil sizzling, waiting to grill.
I am the gill
That lacks the lungs.
The unsung hero.

I have only rescued remedy
Beneath quivering pink tongue.
I am among the graves of your sincerities
With no disparity
Between us.

Religion

We owe our hope to wit: to wit—
Though humor comes as it sees fit.

And long the hours in pain and grit—
Destruction finds to wit: your wit.

CALUMNY

I imagine,
I am a star in the night sky.
So, the bruises of my mistakes—
Smart-less.
To be fair,
They were not smart to begin with.

First Prize

My neighbor has a pullet that won the Pulitzer.

I know he's critically acclaimed,

But I think he has a fowl mouth.

DOG DAYS

I used to think poodles had oodles of time,

But then I spent an hour untangling a curl

And reevaluated.

I've come to the conclusion

That poodles only have oodles of time

If they are Girl Scouts

With an emphasis on knot tying or,

Otherwise, have bondage kinks.

Either way, my mind is quiet again

After much consideration.

Hurt: To Clothe the Cloying

I rest on obscurity.

Pinioned to pinholes—

The moths cloister in my shirt seams,

My pant legs.

Over all the disparaging string,

I ring out fabric in cohesive missives.

My dress addresses the crowd

In flowered, layered lisps—

Lies to itself about the briefness of its hem.

"Too short, too staccato" over stiletto heels

That peel back from ankles after long nights out.

My shouts are held back by briefcases

That lease spaces for my reveries to sit.

I am one pit,

The olive-green jeans forgot to spit back out.

So, I lay about in denim-adjacent duds

Until the suds of self wear thin.

And I grin to clothe myself

In this righteous pelt of skin.

Cater: Present Company Excluded

I am the matron saint of platitudes.
I perform to please but prefer to pill ...
Like fraying linen beneath your thinning fingers.

I cajole and conduct.
It's conducive enough ...
But loneliness still longs to linger.

Automatic

I speak in half sentences
And stuttered out remembrances,
Balling my appendages up within myself.
I take my breath away.
So, they
Cannot acquire it
And stoke some awful fire with it.
I do not owe them ...
Flame.

HORN

I am morally defunct,

A defect diluted by deftness.

I am the hecatomb you atone with,

To appease some pantheon beyond our little god.

I am shod in silent shabbiness.

The skein of my sin slips out of my sleeve.

I weave it into scarves and starve the fabric of necks.

I love to deprive!

I thrive in its scarcity.

I am honor returned.

I am terror and heresy.

Rat Race, Laces Tied

Pitter patter goes the rat.

He is a fat little home-wrecker,

Who swears the curtains caused the kitchen fire

And not the matchbox bed he keeps downsizing

By striking matches against flint countertops.

The rat hates bats—

For rabies sake.

Stakes claim to the attic

Because he thinks he's above you.

There's a dove, too,

Up in the attic,

That he stole from a wedding they held last spring.

It sings him to sleep.

That little creep

Has got it made.

Mind Over

I hit my head on a bird feeder.
I think I left some gray matter
On its edge.

Pity,
I could've used it to figure out
Just where you get the nerve.

Now, there's birdseed in my shoe,
And when I look at you,
It's quite the same discomfort.

What The Sky and I Dislike, Abundance, Confession

There is no life until you pull the sky atop you—

The far-seared glistening orbs,

The broken planes,

Where metal grinds out atmosphere,

The worthless breath in a space drawn from

High-leaping conclusions.

Your orbit, you—

A humble country in a planetary system,

Small and grasping,

To become just like them.

BUSINESS CLASS

There are so many things I want to do:
I want to spell lottery with an "A."
I want to graduate with a degree in liberal arts at the age of twenty-five: *Oh, the humanities!*
I want a post-op postscript from a postgraduate with post-nut clarity (condemned by cocoa butter, again!).

I want to fly business class with nosy middle-aged matrons—your business is theirs.
It's in the name!
I want to die on a hill but have nothing to say,
To hole up with a wholesome wholesaler and pretend capitalism is a grammatical policing (your name here).

I want so very many things.
Rings, sure, if they don't come with a promise.
Hands, if they aren't held too long in flame.
Blame, if it is righteous, and I'm faulty.
Change, if it means things remain the same.

I want so very many things—money, casualties.
War on craziness (my own—indulge me).
I want so very many things—commitment, even.
If you're lucky.

Fog

The fog tugs at my psyche, psyching me out.
(My psychiatrist would have a name for this.)
Sick soldiers of shadows solidified in the silence of
sobriety—I am so aware my eyes can hear the day.

Birds sing sonnets to October,
Hiding in high branches,
Rigid with stage fright,
Tight-beaked around loose notes
That the air adopts willingly.

The ridge of the mountain,
My eyes explore the door to the unfathomable.
I am the substance the earth abuses.
I am the habit, hard-formed in soft times,
Low tones from high minds.
I am the breakdown.

I break through glass ceilings and sever arteries.
Art galleries, hung with paintings of intent.
I lent my last dollar to regret
And owe retrospection my mortgage.
I pay homage to denial and file misgivings with HR,
Stars with five points that never make up constellations.

Syllable Soccer

Elation, the last gift,
The figure of hope,
Rope not yet knotted.
It doesn't have to end up a noose.

Goose-stepping geese.
Grease from stoves kept alive through the night.
Might I can't wield—
Shield me from the portents of paralysis.

Analysis sick and febrile—
Erstwhile days raise hell
In memory banks with no tellers.
Joseph Heller, an insane kind of ruse,
Call it Catch-22.

Blue as my eyes—
Skies I can't fill out,
Shouts in the mist,
Twist the hair at my neck.

Flecks of blood in bile.
At work—
I shirk my sadness to make room for worry.
Hurry life,
Death is catching up.

Poetry

My words are not the soft kind—
Not timid or torn,
Not weathered or worn.
My words are not the soft kind.

They are the waxy waning of the wayward moon—
The sky teeming with birds performing
Rorschach tests for pilots.
They are the bucket that dips into the well.
Well-rounded sentences
That circle back to circumstance
With circumstantial evidence.

Evident in my smile—
The wiles of words fill out resumés to meaning,
Slough off tough facets of myself
By excising the vocabulary
Of feeling.

Cow Choir

Cows chorus doubt—
In the porous drought
Of autumn grain.

Complain—
Of four empty stomachs
and one flummoxed mind.

Bitter to find—
Empty troughs where their breakfast was due,
They moo, and they prattle.

The duty of cattle.
I think they'd be great
(if their breakfast weren't late)!

Esoteric

Socrates dropped his keys
When he was out and about.
Asked five different questions,
In search of directions,
And still hasn't figured them out.

COVID

Footsteps found the sound of removal—
Approval of dinner plates.
Chefs kiss in the backroom,
Perfuming the air with
Love triangles and inner circles.

Square spaces, the chessboard of life represents—
The duality of morality,
The Remus and Romulus,
The Castor and Pullox (the Gemini Agenda).

Amending offending language,
Languid lies told in slow motion.
Devotion devoid and detached.
A match struck against solitude
Inflames the scar of loneliness
That partnership began.

A race ran at break-neck speeds—
Doctors on standby.
Bystanders with high standards
For silverware and cufflinks.
Drinks thrown in bushes,
The philodendron keels over.

God's on sabbatical—
Taking radical action.
"Ecclesiastical self-care"
One HeLL of a face mask.
He tasked it to cover the world.

Belief Grown Stale

Hurt keeps my number in his Rolodex.
Texts "I miss you,"
Like there aren't twenty-five other letters.

I am fettered to the cyclical nature of self-destruction.
The motion of it makes me dizzy.
So, I lay down a moment ...
And rest my head on the safe people.

I steeple my hands, playing pretend,
a politician addressing my constituency.
I've made one too many promises
I knew I couldn't keep.

I sleep with disquiet tangled in my hair.
So, I wear it up in hopes it will not wind
Its way around my neck.

I check the cheeks of my safe people.

They billow out clouds on clear blue days.

Those rays that touch the corners of their eyes,

My lies materialized.

(They think I'm on an upward trajectory.)

They elected me

Daughter/Friend/Sweetheart.

They think my stance is wide enough

To elicit some defense against gravity.

But life bowls me down again,

And I reach for rough people

On my way through the gutter.

In Jest

Adele and Benny Carson had a cow they named Cash.
She ate them out of house and home
And gave Adele a rash.

Cash was spotted black and white
And green around the teeth.
But Benny never looked at them,
For Cash had been bequeathed.

Poor Benny thought the rule he'd heard
About gifted horses' mouths
Applied to cows in equal ways,
And he'd, in looking, turn things south.

But there was more to Cash than met the untrained eye.
For Cash was rich in nuanced milk
That predicted how you'd die!

Just a sip of substance
From that homely cow named Cash
Would tell you if you were to drown
Or have your head be bashed.

The people from surrounding towns
Begrudged the bovine oracle.
And rose a chant one bright May day
You could consider allegorical.

"Thank the good and propitious Lord,
we killed the Cash cow we couldn't afford!"

Fight, Flight, Or Freeze

Tiny wings pulverize air.
I stare at the raw ferocity of flight—I freeze.
I have no fight left in me.

Anika Snyder

Come Sharpen Me, Knife Peddler

I brush my teeth in bed.

(Why not!)

I swallow the toothpaste whole.

(Big gulp!)

I might not be your cup of tea,

But at least I am not dull!

Playing Poker

There is a wobble in my chin.
I lay my palm against it,
Tell it, "Settle down."
It is still for a moment, as if thinking,
Then resumes its shaking.

I feel a surge of loving pity for myself.
Poor child, I think. *Poor girl*.
I sit before the mirror when I cry,
Feeling sorry for myself.

I am a very good listener,
If only for my own sorrows.
Not an hour goes by
That I'm not checking in.

I know each false grin by now
And wag my finger at my reflection.
"It's alright," I lilt in lullaby-adjacent tones.
"Let it out; you can cry."

Oh, how very dear I am to me!
I feed and clothe and bathe myself
And take me on trips.
I never make myself do chores or boring things.
I do not make me wait for anything!

There is a wobble in my chin.
Again, again ... I sin.
That little wobble is the tell
That I forgive.

Syllable soccer

I Could've Been Anyone

There is no disappointment
Like the failure to thrive.
Little glass shoes on tiptoes
So that the tap, tap, tap
Can follow you out the door.

The faces, relatively speaking,
Of the relatives speaking
About your insistence upon mediocrity
Will be wet with grief or rain.

And the pain will bare itself
Up to the surface
Of intelligent eyes with glee.

Thank the good Lord above!
You've covered the whole huggable belly
Of you with stitches and tattoos.
It makes leaving you easier.

The imprint of a hand,
Still visible in red ranging fingers
Across the acres of your skin.

The small grins of your nephew twins,
Jovial witnesses in corduroy
Watch the clock as your grandma hands you
A toy brick to throw through windows
So that the damage that you cause
Is unmistakable.

SYLLABLE SOCCER

I'm Going to Clean my Entire Room

All the artists are starving!
No thank you, plucky pickle—
Your sodium composition is a complete waste on me.
I am five feet seven inches of feral artisan hunger!
My face, the paint you work into dreams at night—
Mold my melon into nightmares,
Smear pretty colors into fabrications,
Prismatic abstractions.
I am so lucky to be your mistress mirage!
Something you forget to tell your wife.
(Get over yourself.)
Strife comes indiscriminately, sour—
It is power to hold the world in the tips of your fingers,
Your tongue.
Let it run out
Like nutrients,
A famished conviction.
All the artists are starving,
As I am.
(What fiction.)

Anika Snyder

There Are Lie Detectors in the Bedroom

I am mean! I bare my teeth—
Gnash my incisors like a tiger.
I am two tons of steel
Or real fiber.
Not the carbon kind of copy
That a lot mistake for sloppy
Attempts at initial models.

I am mean! I scowl and frown and grumble—
No one knows my smile,
Except maybe the miles
Separating you and I!

How I love the distance—
It assures me,
Every lie
Is just a brick to build our house,
Before it crumbles.

The Veneration of (Much Older) Generations

I play the same game with my blood clots
That I used to play with clouds.
I point in excitement! The shapes, almost sounds—
Bunny with one ear, rocket ship, rutabaga,
Colostomy bag, ember, despair!
See there, beside that little ginger hair—
The loss, the love
Forgone and broken.

My mother in her nightgown,
Her legs ungrown and shrunken—
I am five years old;
I want to say.

I wipe her pee in thin streaks off her bathroom floor—
    I am twenty-four to her sixty something.
    And we are awkward in our new grief,
        In the recent way,
        We love each other.

My mother's hip is younger than I am! A new sibling—
    I stick my tongue out at it
    And give my mother gabapentin,
        Pain medicine
        To help with the little twerp.
        "Leave her be!" I coax,
        When we are alone
        And she is sleeping—
    "Let our mother live in peace."

    The tiny infant joint pumps its tiny infant fist.
    Our mother wakes up with a jolt and the gist
        That *I* caused her pain!
        I settle the ice against her skin,
        it's cool refrain, a balm my words

Syllable Soccer

Will never worm their way past.

I am the biggest hurt,
The oldest,
The one my mother has never fully felt or forgiven.
I am on my knees before a sickbed
I never predicted.
I thought she was stalwart,
Unharmed,
Unafflicted.
But her toes are curtains hiding pain.
When they lift,
She screams my name.
I was wrong to think infallible had a human shape.

I think my hips look like hers,
My claves.
I think our eyes catch the light the same.
I think my mother begs me grace,
And I can let her have her way.

Now, I see pockets in my blood clots,
Little hollows to tuck my pride within.
Remember when we were solid? Whole?
Now, you bleed us out and leave us cold.
"I am sorry,"
I say
And cry
And shout.
But it is not enough.
I am withheld—
Without.

My mother
Kindly
Asks after my cramps.
I cannot respond
Because I am in pain.
The shame—
A splinter
That at this same time she is hurting.

The agony, asserting itself
In waves I cannot touch.

There is nothing to relieve—
And if I am no sieve
To her suffering,
I wonder, achingly.
Why have I come here
In the first place.

Henrietta the Hollering Pig

The screams of sows were heard in house.
We trembled at the wailings.
The hooves and tusks
Were shorn and buffed,
Despite the desperate flailing.

Our hearts were moved.
Their bodies, smoothed.
We wish it'd been the sailing.

Health and Wellness

Fear, my prodigal son,
My alien ally,
Who likes to duck
Beneath the arms
Of reason and sense
And infirmly latch
To my gravitized breast.

Fear, my son,
Rises and sets,
Bets against humility for humanity's sake.
I am undone by my ward.
His sword,
Is far mightier,
Than my pen.

The Darndest Thing
(According to me)

I'm a product of embryonic misconception.

Meaning—

They picked the wrong egg to fertilize or insert (IVF).

—God bless you—

I was a pipe dream.

(Oh no! Bedroom fancy.)

I was a hope the pope would holy water the hell out of.

He'd tell my parents to STEER CLEAR ... I'm sure.

Or maybe he'd just duck his head in penitent guilt,

Worried about blasphemous hatred

Or his pituitary gland or ...

Anyways

Syllable Soccer

My mother mismanaged her expectations of Child
And instead got Freak with one too many phobias
And too few,
Let's say, productive inclinations.

It isn't all bad.
I think deadbeat sounds like the end of a song,
The long lingering synaptic riddle
That vibrates with a promise of a next note.

So, yes!
I am that
(Proudly).

I am a product of tectonic commiseration.
I am so moved by the world,
I end up outside of it.

I am the vibration.
Whose migration you can't quite track,
The tact not quite honed,
Just loaned by some didactic deity.
I am my father's.

Favorite.

Failure.

I bet Faulkner would love *that* alliteration.

I am a denizen

And a docent

And the darndest thing—depending on who you ask.

I am rash beyond belief.

(So says my doctor.)

My prescription is 86% domesticity and 14% red wine

That binds time backwards

And me upside down or on my knees.

PLEASE.

Don't ask me questions.

Horticulture

Let my bed be a rose.
Let me rise from said rose.
So, when they say, "She rose from a rose,"
It becomes a sentence bouquet.

And what if *I* were a rose?!
And they could say, "A rose arose from a rose."
And what if there were rows of roses,
Whose toes supposed they were roots,
Who wore little black boots that were beetles,
Who never minded the needles that were thorns,
And never scorned the sharpness of the stem?

And what if you were among them,
With your bright brown eyes
And vaguely disguised love?!
Would you wear gloves to tend my roses and neurosis?
Would you kiss every soft petal,

The red, full of a flower's worth of honey?
Money
Is worth nothing to the bees
And we
Have each other.

Syllable soccer

If I Get Blue on your Shirtsleeve, Leave it for the World to See

I paint my nails badly
To bed down with disaster.
The ridge of old varnish,
Sticking above new—
The hierarchy
Of time.
Replete.
In complete.
Relegation.

I paint my nails badly.
I do not touch the cuticles—
I wander outside the lines;
My skin is pretty.
I leave
The chemicals
To soothe or smother
The natural inclination of my body.

Haughtily, hastily,
I make the paint a waste of me.
The abstraction you turn your head to understand—
The groan of lost art,
The simple aside of seeing new things
In places you knew (the back of your hand).

Syllable soccer

Holding Out For Clarity or Charity, Whichever Comes First

I know a way beyond the sun.
The fever of longing won't last long as jet fuel.
Holding your breath too long makes lions dance on
Gentle imaginings—
The string you tie around me, binding.

I can't fly beyond the sun
Without your relinquishment.

If I am quiet,
You forget me
And loosen your grip.

Now I can float—
Beyond the sun,
Into a place
You can't see
Without hurting.

Nature Break

The nature breaks are meant to provide a little respite from the heavy poems. They are an ode to the wonders of the natural world. My work has brought me ample opportunity for retrospective instruction, carried out by witnessing the delightful way the earth works. I find myself so frequently inspired by the simplicity of the outdoors and deeply indebted to the feeling of expansiveness it provides me.

ANIKA SNYDER

PIECE OF A TIRE ON A LONELY DIRT ROAD

There is a piece of a tire on my lonely dirt road.
I am humbled by its singularity, its fractional pride,
The way it has divided itself up
To be devoured
By hungry eyes.

You get more recognition when you
Outsource your outreach—
When you leave
Fragments
For others to find.
They may carry it with them
If only in mind. But still …
You survive past your boundaries—
And that keeps you
Alive.

STORM

Nothing is boring
In the high wind.
No stale self-sabotaging stillness
Has room to take over.

In the high wind,
The wings of your jacket
Are miles above your head,
Exchanging flight logs with falcons.

The air is glad of its right to life
In the high winds,
And so it sighs
In large sizes
To impress the rocks,
To show them
That it, too,
Can be heavy.

In the high winds,
The smallest secret
Catches itself on tall branches,
Just to fall
Acorn-shaped
Onto earth.

BIRDS (WORDS WITHOUT)

Two finches dart between the parted boughs
Of a sparsely populated apple tree.
The leaves breathe expletives
At the birdbrained pilots as they rush
Too quickly through the few
Green-bodied remains and scatter.
Veined, flat fingers—
Into the heavy autumn rain.

NATURE BREAK

Waves, The Making & Unmaking

I wore a green beanie to work today.
A blackberry bramble liked the stitching,
Or the saturation, and tried to rip it from my head.
I got it back and tossed a pious glance
Backwards at the bullying bush.
We stood fastened to our egos.
Neither of us issued an apology.

Group Effort

It was not the first time it appeared.
The dread fed wisteria to my fears
So that they flowered in pretty little ways.

Look, lay,
Sweet bouquets across the quiet graves
Of our smallest hopes ...
Our deepest desires.

Feed well ... feed long.
Distend sentence to song
So that we all may sway along.

NATURE BREAK

Meaning

Meaning pulls like waves against the strait of self—
The curve of condensation
On a drying soul,
Which hangs its heavy heart on any small thing
Strange enough to dart into view.

BRATWURST

A limb descending onto Earth / The mystery / of breakable things / solved / In the inevitable thunder / I wonder at the way I feel betrayed / The tree / arrayed / Just a second before / In perfect cohesiveness/

And now / the ground has arms / That the tree forgets / or mourns / I hope / for my sake / it's the latter/

I want the world to have a pulse that beats with mine / In time / I suppose / to a sensitive nature / so I wish nature the same / and try and nurture feeling into roots / the way / I wield / conditioner / in the shower /

I will come back tomorrow / and try to find some sadness in the branches / the trunk / just to see / what hurts more /

Leaving /
Or being left behind /

Just Enough

I am livid in the low light—
A decadent hum of harsh mirage
So that your eyes strain from squinting my direction.

I am fifteen leaves and eighty sticks—
Too much and too little,
A wrongness in undescended teeth
That reek at the bursting of raw gums.

I am muscle atrophy—
Emotional apathy.
I am string that frays before it has the chance to knit.
I am solid ground turned into pit!

I sink ...
And seethe ...
And catch you
When you least expect it.

We named it duress

I am gloomy. I am dull. I am a pessimistic person!

This is where you find proof of that.

Take care!

December Seconded My Motion

My blood is a very pretty red
Against the pale of my winter skin.
My index finger,
Spread out from the others—
An ostracism.

My white chipped nails
Invite blood to slither down.
Some morbid Rorschach test
Nail techs would abhor.

It is primal,
This vibrant leak.
I am in awe of my ability
To come apart.

Last night,
I let my left leg freeze
Out in the open air of my bedroom—
No comfort from the comforter.

I keep dissecting myself—
Finger from hand,
Leg from torso,
Just to see what feels like me the most.

Lonely Island PS&G

I am a tiny island, all alone—
A thorn in society's side,
A quiet tide that rises
To consume itself completely.

I am forgotten—
besotted with memory because I lack its favor.
I resolve myself to lingering in corners
Just to see if I am spotted.

If I am—
I remove myself in pieces,
One morsel at a time,
A stripping off of self
Until they see only husk that blows off
In the wind.

I am a tiny island, all alone—
My margins bump boundaries
With nautical whims.
I am set adrift.

When others find me—
They try and make me still,
But their hands slip on my gills,
And my rocks remove their skin.

So, I am alone ...
Again.
Again.
Again.

Little Footsteps Are the Loudest

The other day, the morning was off.
I was a block of wood in traffic cone circles.
I was the worst material for every job I needed done.
I made the insides of my cheeks bleed
With the participation of my incisors,
Biting off more than they could chew.

I made you
A tangle in my heart ...
And batted the hard plastic thing around.
Implausible wreckage ensuing.

I walked seventeen miles, trying to lose myself,
But it seemed I'd been sewn into my body.
I'd like to rip the stitches, even if my fingers tremble,
to find some outlet that lets me out.
So I can seep into the earth and grow correctly.

Born Grief

I am a soap dispenser brimming
With others' expectations.
They fill me up with their liquid
And get angry when I cough it up—
Foam.

I can't seem to get it right—
I ring their coffee mugs
With my suds.
They sigh to see the residue I leave—

No sieve can sort me out.
I'm stuck where they put me.
The blue dawn dimming
With watered-down hindsights.
I am not fulfilling my duty;
They rudely remind me.

I ruminate on the remnants
They refuse to replace.
(I think they are taking their expectations somewhere else.)
I find them at Target,
Buying new soap dispensers.

HUNGER

My face cracks open differently now.
The edges seem full of promise.
No providence divine enough to define
The echoes of protective shape,
The round withering to stone-cold slate,
The clean found within lack,
Within hungering.
The bowl has no depth
That can achieve this ache,
That can reach the envy.
In the eyes of my inner child,
Wide reverence swings out from tree branches.
The bottom of my jeans scuff the dirt.
And I laugh,
Like a lute,
Like a literal instrument!
Dreaming of peppers,
I come awake.

ANIKA SNYDER

Propulsive

Do you exist without it, too?
The towered head.
The vanquished fall.
The flower bed
Without the tall
Stalks and leaves.
The vegetables —
Decidedly delectable

Are you without,
(remiss, remiss)
The very art that you resist?
The taciturn don't turn at all.
They writhe.
They tower.
They fall.
They fall.

Unbidden

The dark hides the rind,
The outside endeavor,
The wall between plenty and null.
The dark is the kind
Of implicit aggressor
That slinks like a scythe
Through your soul.

Diagnosis

Today,
Choice and consciousness
Are my critical comorbidities.

A month ago, I sublet my mind.
For debt and time
Convinced me it was pertinent.

The tenant, Pain,
Brought with it Shame.
Now, my carpet is stained by their union.

Dawning, The Other Thing You Missed

They let me blink by in anonymity.
Proximity.
Screeching,
As the way between,
The middle us
Pretends a non-acknowledgement.

I am on the edge of recognition.
The cognition catch—
As an eye,
A nostril
Reveals some small familiarity.

Didn't I know you?
No.
No.
Never the me you see before you.
You have never met this me.

Anonymity then,
Blameless.
They let me blink by in its calm nothingness,
But they pause and look again
As I am leaving.
So sure now.

Bipolar, As in Kill Me Now

It is divinely approached, this wickedness—
Subconscious and unalterable,
A valley low enough to lay in
And pretend you cannot see the hills.

The fat flat of lack and nothingness
Spit droplets on prophetic words
That sum you up
In geometric ways.
The pastiche of your pathetic life—
All divine.

When you bleed, Plasma (like a screen of indictment)
Screams the things you won't admit.
It is everywhere on you—
The wickedness.
It is in you.
Your witness:

The walls

(All padded now),

Sleep soft again.

Tomorrow, we have divinity to renounce.

How Angular

My jaw is built of flowers
That fall apart in gentle hands.
                        I am a stem too short—
                                  Petal heavy.

Do not touch me like a gathering.
Shake me loose and lose my samplings.

Let me lay seedless and sorry on the dirt.
Let me be driven from desire by destitution and rage.

                        Break my jaw of its bouquet.
                              Set me on a grave.

Endowed

I walk with heavy footfalls.
I take up space,
Reclaim my mass.
You cannot miss me
Or my misstep.
My stumble or sure saunter—
I am the inevitable pounding
On the infinite floor.
When you hear silence,
I have either paused
Or gone
For good.

Between the Tile

I am no more myself—
No more.
The trees forget to blush,
As I traverse their roots.
They cry their leaves
And shake their branches,
But their faces remain placid
At my vastness and unrepentant guilt.
I am built of a bravado
They make birthday candles from.
My wick gets sick of heat.
You blow me out.
I am no more myself—
No more.
They eat the cake.
I lie among the grout.

What I'm Not

I was halfway there—
The almost.
So sweet,
My tongue ached for tang.

I was nearly grasping—
I had the thing in my fingers.
Love was a broken beacon,
A howling hurry up.

As celestial doors rescinded—
Their policy of openness.
There was nothing left,
Only dirt and grime and rot.

And who was I
But a shadow,
Shouting questions at shapes.
Asking.

Do you love me?
Do you like me?
Do you hate
The way I move?

With
No answer
Big enough
To believe.

ANIKA SNYDER

Bricks and Straw

I am mesh and tin foil hats
And every square bit of cardboard
You abhorred for its presumption.
I am mass and diminutive glances.

I graze past elbows
And bowl *myself* into the gutter.
I am cast aside by sideways tensions.
The length of disapproval fits along my wrist.

I am ribboned
And ribald,
Rambling gambles of emotions
When I feel dead inside.

I have talked myself out—
Of every hole
And hold
I've been in.

And still
Feel their teeth
In my back.

WE NAMED IT DURESS

BONE BROTH

I am five years old again today.
I have little legs.
Little arms.
Little eyes.
Little ears.
I have a very little voice.
So, you have to listen close
To hear my fears.

ANIKA SNYDER

Our Youth

It wasn't just the Big Dipper and anonymity—
Some wish the stars would make.
It was the sour summer sun,
Thrashing itself on moon residuals—
The outlandish pond we were fond
 Of getting lost against.

We'd bump our tired backs
Into ridiculous propositions,
Our fingers decked out in candy jewelry,
With our newly fashioned faiths.

We were bated breath
And wheat-pleated tongues,
Wearing sandwich murals
Across our white picket teeth.

WE NAMED IT DURESS

We were five inches
From growing into ourselves,
And we basked
In that youthful shade.

So excited for change,
We didn't realize
What we had
Until we lost it.

Anika Snyder

How Could I Complain?

The way the skin has room for me—
Reaches gladly for consult,
For consumption,
Some compliment
Of underfed appetite.
The way I stretch towards
Reward!

Skin, a broken house—
Windows shuttered,
Gutters filled,
A thing I find no home in
Until I tear it
From the beams.

How I seem agitated,
Like steel wool across red knuckles,
Like a fist swallowed by a mouth
That lets no words escape.

WE NAMED IT DURESS

I am the last great ape,
The primitive pleasure,
The pain, uninspired
But felt to the bone.

An inchoate elocution,
Spoken so softly,
Not even the speaker
May know.

Anika Snyder

If Only Briefly

Broken, then—
Hard up.
Weary.

A chair pulled back from table—
Peeled even,
Solitary.

Where has bravery been—
Some far coast without a leg?
The wooden sitting down to eat,
Stiff maple for teeth.
Oak for eyes.
No allotment of surprise,
Too sweet to swallow.

Only the just—
The chair from table.
Alone, sure.
Broken and worried.

But waiting—
Held breath in a knotted spine,
To be impressed upon,
If only briefly.

Jolly

I am the practiced pit that puts the plum to shame,
The pulmonary pull inside a fractious skin.
I am the only grin you use in times of discomposure.

I am the hidden gem with rutted caves that coddle fear.
I am alone along the proper edge you tear,
Just me and my deficiency,
The fruit will rot me sick.

Anika Snyder

Up, As in Time's

I keep looking up,
Hoping the answers will drop from the sky,
Like ticks from the trees
And nestle into my hair—
Trying to slip past the
Bare barrier of my skin
Into the dim
Cavern within.
Light me up in kerosene flames
And suck my life away.
Knowing does that to people—
I've seen it.
It drives you insane.

Psych Ward (Pearly Gates)

In the psych ward there are many evils.
There is violence
And silence.
There is cowering
And showering
Behind "doors"
That are half measures of the things
You never knew you'd miss so much.

In the psych ward they confiscate your ego
And the strings of your sweatpants,
Replacing glasses with paper cups
That rupture under too much pressure.
You are likely to relate to them.

In the psych ward, the ambiance of screams
Seems a lullaby you'll never quite get used to.
But in time,
You might find
The variance of pitch
Scratches an itch in your sick, sick brain.

And that primal refrain
Becomes a rallying cry
That you believe
Will leave
You behind
If you ignore its call
Too long.

In the psych ward, you are pinafored and frocked,
Some antiquity shopped
From the none too distant past.
In the psych ward, you find nuance in the shock
Of cold feet in borrowed socks.
Their grip holds longer
Than yours
Will last.

My Very First Baseball Game

I, in my stadium seat
Alone. Alone—
Despite a cluster of people beside me ...
The sun, a refracted accusation
Through beer-blind eyes
Irrefutable brightness with no clarity.

How am I alone?
The tone, the whimper
Of awareness
Of otherness
In a sea
Of collective understanding.

The knowing, a lifted finger, a rigorous chant
A standing ovation—
The observation of correct posture for a throw.
A fight amongst the brave, bold boys
Like stretched out children
Old enough to scream and melt the mountains.

Would I be escorted out
If I acted just as they have?
Is the net, the field, the prospect of sport
Enough to twist undefinable sociality
To the favor of the spectator—
To the gladiator fun
Of watching people devolve.

No.
I would be a threat. A menace. A fear.
And they would take me away—
For good. For good.
So, I stay in my chair,
Look aghast through my hair—
I, in my seat ...
Alone.

Alone.

OUTREACH, ON LONELINESS & DESPERATION

I have been very lonely lately. I live in a little room in a big house full of people. I have been very lonely lately. The little room is a little cold at night, so I hug my little dog close. He is seven pounds and generates as much heat as angry words or passionate dissertations. My little dog does not like other people, so we isolate, like lightning in its last attempt at showing up—one bold, brilliant streak and then void. The other night, I heard footsteps outside my window—harsh, loud, scary, and I couldn't help but wish they'd stop on by.

ANIKA SNYDER

The Puzzle Piece Lost Under the Couch

I was not born intact.
I was born in two,
A twin that tore behind my sister
A mere minute after her birth.
Scared, even then,
That she would leave me behind.

I find myself bracing,
Left palm to my forehead,
Right held to hers,
To feel if the fever of living
Has infected her
As it has me.
If the free enterprise of experience
Has taxed her as unexpectedly.
If the labor of love bends her frame the same,
And if she lacks
The proper prescription
To aid in unobstructed foresight.

I was not born intact,
In fact, I believe our division splintered wrongly—
So that the one pound, one ounce of her
That was more than me
Was the part of me she took.

WE NAMED IT DURESS

In books, I found the outline of that part,
But it felt like water in a wicker basket,
Dripping slowly or quickly—
Depending on the viscosity.
The stone-cold facts
Seemed to last the longest.

My twin and I, Sarcophagi,
Entombed in our destruction.
I exploded outwards.
She imploded inwards.
We both lay waste
To something others wanted whole.

I broke hearts and walls and watches,
Whose glinting heads I couldn't face.
She broke heart
And bone
And body
And became the only loss I couldn't take.

I excelled in separation because ours was so vast
That any successive parting was a lit candlewick,
Sputtering beside a forest fire.
I was in dire need of connection,
But the collection of those I used to fill the void
Toyed maliciously with the edges of her absence.

There is no substitute for the other half of you.
There is only patchwork,
Like a Band-Aid on a boat's body,
Letting water gather, ravenous, around impassive feet.
The patchwork people promise
Respite from the mourning.
But they never know quite why
You shroud yourself in black.
And in time ...
It takes more effort
To conceal their inadequacy
Than to lose them to the world.

And so, I let them go ...
One by one,
Like the separate ashes of our grandmother
That we scattered across two coastlines.

And I could never mourn their leaving,
Even if I tried.
Pressing the heels of my hands against my eyelids,
Wishing my eyes
Were eggs over easy
So that the blue of my irises could pop
And pour down my gracious cheeks,
Sapphire tears to leer at heartbreak.

WE NAMED IT DURESS

Was I remiss?

I never spoke of my need for her.
Sometimes, my need was quiet.
But sometimes, my need clamored and clawed
Its way out of my scream-weary throat,
Transforming, midair, into insults that surprised us both
with the keenness of their cruelty.

How could I harm that which I held most dear,
Pushing away the thing my arms felt empty without?
Devout as I was,
I became a terrible follower,
A congregant singing hymns off-key to ruin a harmony,
A cult member stoutly refusing my Kool-Aid.

I paid for my transgressions,
For the words
I didn't mean to say
But couldn't get back
Even when I asked her
Nicely for them.

She was out our childhood door
More rapidly than wine down thirsty throats.
The coats she supposedly outgrew
Became sour with the scent of disuse.

And some days, when I felt her absence terribly,
I'd slip my arms into sleeves
That used to wind their fabric across her skin
And feel for a shimmering, soft-scented second
That I was the twin with extra parts,
Instead of the one missing them.

I was not born intact,
I lacked
Some fundamental wholeness.
I was an O turned to a C,
A circle that could not close itself.
When we were three, then six ...
My sister closed that circle for me.
She became the piece
To fix my lack of fullness.

But now, somehow ...
I think that piece of hers is mangled
And dangles at an angle,
Like a broken ulna bone.

I know one too many people
Who think that they can
Break me,
But I was not born intact,
And now I can't be
Reassembled.

This Isn't What I Meant

This isn't what I meant.
The order—
Like a symptom
Of an inexhaustible mind.
How to find great expectations
Beyond belied belief.

Neat trickles of freckles—
Showing up unkindly
on ear tips and wings.
The argumentative approach—

What. Did. You. Do.

Name accomplishments—
Laundry
List
Laundry
List

How fantastic ordering can be
When done inexpertly.
The stretch
Of Thinking.
To be feeling just alright—
And jump into dread
Unaided.

AND AFTER THAT, WHO KNOWS

My hands are swollen—
pulpy, red.
The heat,
A cask I leave behind.
I drink from reservoirs inside
And bloat and bloat
To float up to the clouds.

The feet disturbed,
Blood blister: few knew how it formed.
Dirty for police run-ins, more and—
Out of time before
Hospital stays.
Handcuffed
To The Way I Used to Be.

That sick, haunted beast—
In alleyways,
In bushes,
Hidden.
The ants, even,
Climbing up each others' backs
To set off light sensors.
"She's over here!"
I race away.

A heartbeat and a signal now—
The redlight and the sun.
The heat I have begun to feel.
My hands swollen, swollen,
My tongue.
Rough energy sucked—
The sides raw razors
They'd strip from me.
My sightless unforgiving nails,
The carver
With stick upon his knee.

Under highways—
Some far mile away,
The feeling coming back ...
Coming back.
The tingling:
With cessation, when I still.
And after that, who knows.

WE NAMED IT DURESS

COVERED ARENA

In a singsong or a lilt—
The birds all make reply.
The sky is fabric.
The clouds, metal rods.
There are one ...
Two ...
Three pairs of wings.

The sun is a hundred fluorescent lights.
Number ninety-one is broken—
And hangs
Like a split lip,
Ripping itself in two.

The birds make a nest in its gums—
The sun will not turn on again.
It's dark in here.

I'm numb.

Anika Snyder

In The Corners of The Room

Two things are silent now—
The picture frames,
You.
I am awake beside contrition,
Aware of the state of my soul.
The whole flammable assembly of it—
How it burns.

I have made a turn too far now,
So lie in a bed I haven't made.
I should have stayed home
But have come too far with loneliness.
So, I put it down again—
On a mattress with protestations on its lips.
The tips of hair just barely visible
Above my ego.

The resounding sound of hollowness,
In the crook of an arm—
The minutia of the minutes like minotaurs that gouge
Me to extinction.
The timing of it all,
Awake in indecision.
Who am I now?
The jury will not decide.

Case Number

The things that you deny—
The kit that doesn't come with tape,
That will not repair
But dissects the things that have happened to you
In the last
24 hours.

How amazing modernity seems
In the wake of such antiquated injury,
The system lined with metallic ways to find the source
Of pain—
The needles gain the blood you divulge in gasping
Cries.
Please believe me,
The vermillion villains
Plead and perform for the nurses.
Try, try to be known as true—
The last inclination of survival,
To be understood.

The valiant forging forward—
Even as
The body shutters
Under warmed hospital covers and kind words.
It was not your fault.
Why then?
Why?

Anika Snyder

The Skin of Soggy Skies

I am rain-wrecked and tired,
Uninspired even—words forget my name.
I leave my curtains the same,
Drawn, like me.

The rain hates their exclusivity
And howls it's pain
Through tree branches, runoff creeks
That leak
The lie of follow through to bitter ends.

I send—
Myself to their edges,
Rain-wrecked and tired.
Peer in, the fronds are fond of catastrophic things—

They smiled at me today.

How I Deprive Myself

I should be getting back to you
AnyDay!
I think my Wi-Fi is slow,
My fingers stiff from winter.
I will get back to you
AnyDay!

I find it curious
How lonely
I am.
And yet refuse(!)
To answer people.
It is like feeling hunger and sewing your mouth shut.

AH ...

There it is.

I Have a Very Orange Sweater

I have a very orange sweater.
It is brighter than my smile on sunny days!
I wear it so that no one pays attention
To how dull I feel.

Yesterday, at work,
My coworkers all joked
That they would not lose me in a storm.
I blinked my hurricane eyes,
Pursed my earthquake mouth,
And wished to all things natural (disasters included)
That they were right.

And I Wonder Where I'll Be

My lungs are shifty fellows.
They bellow out belief
Before I have the chance to censor sound.
I run aground in accusations,
My either oar—
A paddle I raise only to strike myself.

I see the glinting gold of madness
In the sadness I adopt.
My tears turn my duvet a funny shade of white—
Some off-color joke
At the expense of my heartbreak.

I am very, very young.
But what good is this youth,
When I waste it
In such predictable ways?

Anika Snyder

When The Storm Comes By

My ears are hidden from the storm—
A thin piece of fabric
Cradles the soft pink flesh,
A tender appraisal
Of organic matter
Made fallible
By harsh elements.

There is no running in this weather.
My feet are frozen to the spot.
I rot in my rain boots,
Like cake in the fridge.
The ridge of my icing,
My
Self
Is tinged green.

If you see me coming,
Wonder why your stomach turns—
When I lean
Against your arm—
The storm issues my decay.
I lay my weight on figments
And imagine myself
Away.

I Am Not Afraid of Heights

I worry deep, deep down,
But it bubbles to the surface.
I am in service to my fear.
I am too short to see over it,
So, I slip into it
Instead.

What It's Not

It could be the head of
A closed tulip
With a stuffed duck's bill
Atop its petals.

It could be
Pumpkin-lanterned lights slung
Seasonally along the end seam
Of a perpetually broken
Sliding glass door.

Or

A speculum
Swung
In disinterested efficiency
At the root of a tree
That forgot it had its footing.
A masochistic need
In other news
To rid termites from its bark.

WE NAMED IT DURESS

"Open wide!"
The doctor urges.
Tremors in knees.
Roots pull apart.
(Cry squirrel, why jay?)
The sap will out.
It is not a tree.

Favorite song

Coffee shop ... stoppered in on all sides by eyes I do not recognize. Shapes. Seemingly kind, the vines of others' lives twining with shuttering relief against the thick walls of humanity. To be held in shared space, to breathe air stretched to bursting with flavor—yeast and coffee beans, indole and the high sweet scent of imminent common colds. A sneeze away from damp. Perennial showers. The power of a napkin as it wipes away the tear slipped sideways down a thickened cheek. The seeking in the loudness all around, where my silence propounds its immensity. The lily pad on a stagnant pond, waiting for landing—or something else green to quell the loneliness.

My Voice is Young; I Lost it As a Child

Is there a carved-out place for innocence to sit?
I could let it rest awhile
And pick it up—restored, grown.
Maybe just a corner—
Somewhere soft enough to sleep …
Something that seeps into the gentleness
I lost so long ago.

Is there a carved-out place for innocence to sit?
Having it with me
Is like carrying a dandelion
Through a heavy storm.

Nature Break

The nature breaks are meant to provide a little respite from the heavy poems. They are an ode to the wonders of the natural world. My work has brought me ample opportunity for retrospective instruction, carried out by witnessing the delightful way the earth works. I find myself so frequently inspired by the simplicity of the outdoors and deeply indebted to the feeling of expansiveness it provides me.

ANIKA SNYDER

For Mica Or Steel, Whoever Swings First

Her footsteps are slow / panther paws in wet dirt / her
Collar sings itself a riddle / she is waiting for the
Mountains to give her prey / my leash, the only way she
Stays / bound to me, unmoving.

We trudge ourselves to grass / the valley below is mist
City / little suggestions of cows in the clouds / I take
Pity on the shroud of clarity / and pretend
I cannot see its loss.

I am out of breath / and she beneath me / seizes on my
Weakness/ fills her mouth.

NO MATTER / I count to five / she is remorseful /
Regurgitating me in one hiccupping spew / her yellow
Eyes bleat sorry / her tender tongue a mew / I forgive
Her / her transgressions / just as I have you.

Nature break

The Uses Of Water

Spillways and stillness
Almost—

The storm
Almost—

Noise.

I carry water on my back.
The weight,
A waiting.

A thing contained until consumed,
A confirmation of a use
It did not know it had.

The spillway,
Jealous-eyed
At the backwater.

The promise
Of something
Minutes away.

ANIKA SNYDER

Father's Day Gander

We ordered two geese,
Instructed a crate to contain
The ruffled feathers.

Three came for the price of two.
We gawked.
The stock of thin beaks.
Hisses, seeping like sprung leaks
From orange fastenings.

The heat, a caress with sharp ends,
Smoke thick on rioting winds.
A June day devoid of calm in California,
The promise of something bad
Waiting in the wings for its cue.

NATURE BREAK

IN THE SKY

Like a gathering storm—
The orange stroke
Ripped
Across the sky
Like genius.

Ideas were clouds
That cauterized
The harshest edge
Of sunrise.
Broke molted tendrils
Of vapor
From the tapestry
It came from.

The road
Was a symposium for concrete concerns,
Mainly beauty's indiscretion—
How it spread
In such indecent ways—
Exposing
Its immensity
Like an unchaste icon.

My fingers were fond of the first light.
The way the warmth of color
Splashed on empty nails.
Margins filled by natural poetry.
Making the heaviness
Of hands
Nearly weightless
When raised
In enraptured idolatry.

Assets With Assistance

In the petals of the morning,
My fingers find their home.
Taut tendons teeter on each precipice they meet.
The fleeting press of feeling
In the joining of my worlds.

In the petals of the morning,
I let the light rise above me—
Sustain itself like music: an ideology.

In the petals of the morning,
I begin anew.
I am hanging from the rafters
In a stiff bouquet,
A revision left to dry
From the rain.

Mendocino

The wasps on the low lake sand assault the rocks.
The water sops
The stillness with its gentle lapping—
Lopping
Wet fingers
Through muddied breaches.

Branches
Of dead things—trees, imaginings—
Layer the small cove, cover my growth
In eulogistic silencing.
The intonation of life lived
In the absence of its muttering.

I, still quiet,
Sit beside the beauty. Wonder
If it truly matters
That I fit no setting better.
This, the only place I need—
The mud, the dead things sighing,
The wasps on the rocks,
The water watching.

NATURE BREAK

And calm I find this—
The figure, a loneliness
That pierces even
The subtlety of nature.
A silhouette on a distant shore
You can't be sure
You see.

But there I am,
Grown in the mountainside.
Trail marks
Along my thighs—
Majestic
And awful
But free.

Hydrant or Hydrangea, Dogs Aren't Discerning

Verdant landscape beyond
Stretch ...
Fine minutia in the dust we forget ...
The countless twinning leaves,
Seamless branches!
Truncated.
Translucent.

A Utopic whim of amnesia:
To mislay the information provided.
The bare land,
A flash of vision away.
One or two?
One or two?

Pick the lively,
The new.
The rose-colored glasses
Look best on you.

NATURE BREAK

When Things Start Making Sense

The shrubs and grass are green for a spell—
It is almost June in California.
The moon hangs itself up every night
Like a first-place prize.
The owls shriek through molten beaks
That break the air in hot polemics—
The paltry parliaments
That need some getting used to.

The shrubs and grass are green for a spell
On the mountain trail.
The top is yellowed,
But in the shade,
The rays of light
Cannot bleach them.

I hover over the stems, the roots.
I give them soft names for their honor.
The horror of anonymity will not tear them from me.
The shrubs and grass are green for a spell.
I am very good at counting.
The things I count on are like the shrubs and grass
And don't last long.
I think I know now
What the owls are screeching for.

Men (Swearing, power steering, & me)

I'm sorry, Mom. I'm sorry, Dad. I'm sorry, men who think me good when I've been bad! I'm the worst kind of romantic (nearly not at all) but here are poems to immortalize the fallen.

Rent

Love and art. The unconquerable things—
We are rudimentary kings,
Who rule the way between them.

Our kingdom is divided up in half—
You take the side of love.
I take the side of art.
Both of us covet what we cannot touch.

APROPOS OF NOTHING

Apparently,
(This may come as a shock—even I am surprised),
I am not the center of the universe.

It is not even about me loosely
(Or about me being loose)!

It is not concerned with my words or my actions.
I am a forgotten piece of so many days!

I can bask in that ray of glory for a while.
I move differently in anonymity; it makes me smile.

For the Breeze, Don't Shoot!

I worry my lip (for nothing)!
I'm fine; I sign to the mirror, the walls,
Anything tall enough to look me in the eye—

Fine!
A piece of paper with regret written across its pale face.
The grace of hands imprinted on my visage.

Like vision obstructed by grains of sand—
How blind my little irises,
How mistaken.

I awaken to my gut in utter knots of intuition!
What a pretty dream I've had, my dear.
I know. I know. But it felt so real!

MEN (SWEARING, POWER STEERING, & ME)

MY KNEES

I see baby faces in my knees and in the moon.
But you only swoon at one of them (not my knees).
I don't know how her perfect roundness is pleasing
And mine offensive, but we'll get to that eventually.

My knees are multipurpose.
They buckle, bend, saunter—lift, lope, stand me up
At half my height,
Which is just the way you like me.

My knees run, romp, pray,
Ache, grow, part.
(I find it funny you delight in their divorce.)
It must be some cosmic joke, those faces in my knees.
Like I have three minds, three sets of molars and
Morals.

I must make God laugh when I run.
Three-headed,
Arms pumping,

Though I don't think it would be laughter at my form.
Just the thought of me thinking
I could get away.

As for roundness, mine.
Hers: I've come to understand
That you need her full to function.
Because her light lets you see
Just how much you've starved me.

Around Yours

I have a necktie
That I use
For special occasions—
Funerals, decapitations,
Anything I can't quite wrap my head
Or arms
Around.

The necktie is a vivid forest green—
Sharp and clean,
Like pine needles
Or the sheen of unshed tears in youthful eyes.

The necktie is used to knots.
So, it takes criticism in stride
When I tell it ...
It is not.
Allowed.
To.
Lie.
It understands.

I treat every man
Like my necktie.
I use them for special occasions—
Funerals, decapitations.

I expect them to take criticism in stride
And tell them they are not allowed to lie.
Their faces are hollow graves.
They say they'd rather die
Than save the truth for me to suck on.

So, I purse my lips and spit my teeth

Their way.

MEN (SWEARING, POWER STEERING, & ME)

ICARUS

You push outward,
Furious.
I am a study in internal organs.
I run my finger across my pancreas,
Playing at placidity.

You hook me in,
Up
A fish that cannot wriggle free.
Me,
A dangle at the end of your dangerous conclusion.

I sour slightly.

Milk white in the sight of the dour inheritance.
The dowry of your anger
Favors shapes I cannot fathom.
I'd rather random bits of fluff
Than this toughness in demeanor.

Than our brooms at war with wind—
We cannot clear the air.

Nominated

I wrote a road eroded.
I made the coming apart seem swift.
I made rifts
Between concrete
Seem
Complete in their dysfunction.
I made delusion seem delightful.
I made selflessness seem spiteful.
The biggest sleight of tongue,
It's true,
Is making love turn into you.

Men (Swearing, Power Steering, & Me)

GG

I am glamor and glimmer,
Glory and gore.
I am loose with my body,
So they call me a whore.
I'm a siren, a saint,
A sinner that snores.
I am all of these things,
But I'm never a bore!

Anika Snyder

Slut Shame, Kissing too Many Frogs

This is tantamount, I can't amount to—
Who you want me to be:
A proper girl who sits, legs crossed,
Around mixed company.

I bump a knee against a man's
And smile with flashing teeth.
He slides his eyes down to my cans–
His sword falls out its sheath.

A thief of hearts, whose own is cold—
I shudder to admit it.
I flirt and kiss, yet still I'm told,
Princes never ribbit.

MEN (SWEARING, POWER STEERING, & ME)

JEALOUS! SEE WHAT I CAN DO

My legs are frogs' legs.
Pushing
Up,
Up,
Up.

Jumping to lily pad conclusions,
Whose green hue
I turn into.

Jealousy's prosperity—
No rarity in my eyes.
(You'd think with age it would have gotten softer.)

But I adopt her—
Mannerisms
To make you smile bigger.

And get sicker,
When I realize
That it's working.

Playing It Koi, A Picture-Perfect Pisces

I am a pseudonym suitor,
Tutoring the suited I've recruited—
Teaching them the way to move their tongues,
So I can hear a name that is not mine
Slip off their lips.

I am a pseudonym suitor,
Cuter for the mystery
That my dissolving history provides me.
The key to anonymity is the ability to disregard
Identity without enmity or fear.

To tear tears from the eyes
Of your own mother
Because you do not want to be you anymore.
At the core of self I discovered,
I hovered metal detectors across its depth.

Men (Swearing, Power Steering, & Me)

No gold leapt up,
So I crept up
To language
And asked it to save me.
It renamed me.

And I became the thing
That rings with newness
In such an imperceptible way,
You can't go a day
Without thinking of my smile.

To Deal In Extremes

I split the difference between deference and derision—
The decision,
A kind consensus after contentious rebuking.

A lofty moral—
Held below the lips of another
Until you can't quite tell
Which was tender,
Which was tough.

It is enough
To find the middle ground
And to forget how to wonder—
To preserve the peace of halfway,
In an effort to be good.

MEN (SWEARING, POWER STEERING, & ME)

GRASS AND WHATEVER STICKS TO IT

Precious little is preposterous on a precipice.
There is no limit to denial
Or flagrant fantasies of reprieve.

You feel the wind blow in the objectively
WRONG direction—
Blow softer, please curl past my elbow!

There is no crushing you escape on the edge.
The ecclesiastical hammer
Will flatten you entirely.

A speeding car,
A shout that hollows you out,
A vacancy of self,
In a once occupied body.

The absorbency of a decades old shirt
That steals away the tears
That traipse in twos down reddened cheeks.

There is precious little propriety on a precipice.
The once loved in skins are turned hateful and old.
A youthful death of happiness—the cold.

A bitterness where hope should be.
A frightened howl,
Blind refusal to reduce an apoplectic rage.

He was soft to me,
And now he's vengeful.
Now he cuts along my edges,
And we fall from grace.

Noon Tomorrow

By noon tomorrow—
You'll forget my lips.

The sips of beer
Between broken dreams
That seem
Abundant in the moment—
That fall to fantasy in morning.

I mourn the mystery
Of the second before confession.

The light—
In bright blue eyes
That sings of love
Before it's spoken.

Pew, Pew

They don't know me where you're from. They would shiver at my underbelly, the undulating unctuousness of my ugliness. The dice that cower. The cowardice. My unlucky roll. Your snake eyes slither down my body, land a centimeter off from soul. You are not shape. You do not shift. And, so, you never see—who I really am.

Men (Swearing, Power Steering, & Me)

Holy Scripture

See where you land—
Far off,
Spun out,
Wriggling under some
Torn off image.

The book begs its binding back,
Shoves you away—
The page who couldn't turn,
In service of heavy words.

I moved my eyes across your depth
And found all the many syllables
Couldn't add up to profundity.

ANIKA SNYDER

THE HILL WE DIE ON

There was very little in the last words.
Everything had fallen out,
Watered down and drowsy.
You lifted a hand
And at the last moment
Remembered
That my knee was out of bounds
And that we,
Nebulous and shaky,
Were connected only by proximity.
No longer the shade of relational bliss,
The plainness of truth
Sweltered in shelters we swore to forsake.
We were remiss and remote,
Throats fissured with unmiraculous vowels—
You said I.
I said you.
We sought consonants
And came up inconsolable.

Visionary

I have had huge hands
My entire life.
I tip ever so slightly towards the ground.
I almost never have my hands full
Because of their capacious capacity.

My fingers are five feet long—
My nail beds are king-sized
At the very least.

My knuckles would buckle the most fearsome fighter.
This has been the whole of my existence,
Though my resistance to gloves has recently changed—
Because you fit your hand around mine,
And twine a smile through my hair
And just stare at how small my fingers look
Beneath yours.

How Then

Am I supposed to play with the light of your words forever? Twist my knuckles through your instruction: "Keep it up," you say.
But I'm sure you are joking. Because the mist of your spit. Lands between my eyes. And somehow. I can see. What you mean now.

Men (Swearing, Power Steering, & Me)

On The Worship of Wooden Icons in a Fire-laden Land

I've been trying to dismantle my pedestals as of late.
I find
That the fall
From such high heights
Leaves my icons
Too bruised
To reconsider
(Spots on avocado, soft mush behind each peel).

Reading Richard Brautigan's
Trout Fishing in America—
I am mouth-agape astounded at the way he twines his
Words to the wonder of the world,
Finds soft things and humor on the cusp of universal
Humanity.

How he Gets it—the big picture, small miracle,
Instruction of nature.
The order, so precise, we cannot extricate ourselves
From its lesson.

And then he cums in a stream—
Among dead fish.
And he is just a man to me,
Like every man that came before.
And his mark is rough on the edge of my vision.

He is just a man—
And he begs no softness from the land
but for the places he digs to bury himself in.
To plant parts of existence in callous ways—
Like sperm in running water,
Heading off the current,
Sweeping my idols away.

MEN (SWEARING, POWER STEERING, & ME)

BRANCH

The pale endings of breath, where they caught—
Like wind in butterfly nets, the exhalation
Of my worry.
Came butter smooth over the hills,
To land
In the hair
Of a forearm
Essential to
My steadiness.

It jerked back—
I felt the movement like a laceration.
And beneath that, the blood
Pooled in unseemly coagulation.

To Be Light Again

I can lay my full self into you—
Which I haven't done since I was small.
I can lay my full self into you—
And not think about my heaviness at all.

Men (Swearing, power steering, & Me)

Pity the New

You will be no brief grief.
You will consume me,
But as I am undone,
I am reborn.

Envoi:

It was the briefest grief
I've ever known,
A feather flown
On tepid wind.
He was not worth
The weight of thought.
I am so glad
I'm done with him.

ANIKA SNYDER

Leaving (How Many Times?)

My knuckles are much too large
For my small, small mouth.
I spit them out—
My joints are lined in flame.
My nails are half polished with varnish,
Half with saliva.
I am snail-like
And slimy—
I leak like the faucet
I rinse myself out with.

The toilet is grimly grimy,
My younger self would have cringed
At how I am unwinding.

My knees are Play-Doh soft—
The bones are jutting through.
On the ledge of the tub there is a long, black hair
Curled like a mouse
In winter.

My mouth is emptying.
My hands are trembling.
I leave my key in a small palm.
I've forgotten how I held.

Men (Swearing, power steering, & Me)

Left Behind

I left a few things behind.
I left my jacket and my mug—
The one I was very smug about drinking from
Because it was bigger than the rest of them.

I left it for you because
I have plenty now.
Without any need
For substantive matter,
I am enough
In myself.
And that's the best divorce of assets
I could ask for.

Sickness and Its Witness

Forgive me my infirmness,
My bodily debility,
The tightness in my lungs—
The way
They
Strain
In ways
They shouldn't have to.

Excuse the dissolution.
(Forgive, forget.)
I will be perfect soon!
The phlegm will clear.
The eyes will dry.
The slick slime of my sickness will
Slide off my shoulders!

Forgive me my infirmness,
Though I think I love you more now
For your witnessing
my feebleness.

MEN (SWEARING, POWER STEERING, & ME)

TO THE ULTIMATE END

Desolate, denizen of denial,
A township brokered by wayward asides.
The questioning foreplay of grand actions, like
Leaving—for good.

Who would miss the rueful smile?
The limbs splayed—
Over comforters, apologies.
The gangly veins bulging at temples,
Filling with the viscous remnants of dishonesty.
The lies, little blue floaters in bluer irises,
Almost indistinguishable.

Still, the truth of it.
The wrongness in the teeth,
Gnashed together in an approximation of joy.

Joy then falsely represented,
Something like hatred in the midst of a gaze.
The sunlight slanted through a gap in the curtains
Touching, softly, the endings of us.

The toes now, our words,
Bookends and brokenness.
The bay of our sadness—
Docked in and docile.
Swallowed, as things tend to be
The second we turn away.

Men (Swearing, power steering, & me)

Helmets and Hornets

He had me by the hand.
I had a little left in me.
I ran ahead—
Trying to fit the night around me,
Like carved meat around a blade.

I splayed,
Wrought-iron fingers
Across grass blades, houses—
Made.
The world domestic,
In protected vision.

The back of my shirt—
Caught on a breeze.
Then his nails
Snagged on presumption.
On a safety
He could never
Guarantee.

Anika Snyder

Blinds On All Sides

Smoke sold by distracted lungs
To the cold afterthought of night.
Hands exchange damage and fire,
Irrespective of each other.

A thin stick, a folded prayer for relief—
In small hopes without distinction.
Alone, blind faith in altered states, golden domes that
Deign to convert into mosquito netting for our fears.

We are safe,
Solemn,
Drunk on the sidewalk
Outside your old apartment.

We are stars—
And the couch
Has arms to catch our heat.

I burn out first—
Head on something unlike you but so much the same.
Sleeping
And believing
This could still be us.

MEN (SWEARING, POWER STEERING, & ME)

A Mania Unshelved

His hands cracked open.
I hid beneath the bed, the closet—
Walked across the ceiling beams,
Listening for radio chatter.
Looked over the balcony, imagining falling.

My eyes were moon-sized—
Golden, glowing
Orbs absorbed in the way the dust motes molted.
His hands, orange from my hair—
Scrambled like eggs across my back,
My arms,
My legs,
As I slipped
like silk
Through his fingers.

I was smoke—
Across the carpet,
In the pages of a Ken Kesey book.
Finally,
In the cracks of his hands,
He ensnared me.

ANIKA SNYDER

Fury, Too Fast?

I dress you up in quiet kisses.
Your sarcastic skin laughs to be impressed upon
And leaves no mark visible.

I trace the map of my mouth on the world of you—
And find nothing but the gentle damp
Of my unceasing love.

The decision, like a drop of dew
To cling to that which will uphold it—
For a little while.

MEN (SWEARING, POWER STEERING, & ME)

JUST YOU AND PANTHERS

It is no fair.
The bears play so lightly—
Some tinkling laughter,
Some rumbling two-legged stance.
A glance of avuncular joviality—
No sinister dimension like
Locked doors or
Panther paws.

It is no fair.
I have been given panthers.
Their lethal bearing,
Something grizzlies couldn't fathom.
I place my little hands behind my back.
There is no fighting this—
The claws, the teeth.
I am in bits before they drag me back to you.

Anika Snyder

Lock (No Key)

It clicked.

(Click!)

The size of all my fears, that sound.

The resounding doom of its promise of barricade,

In the do not disturb of its brass bones

That make my bones

Believe they've lost their marrow.

How do feet forget to move?

My lip can tremble—

My hands can stroke

The sides of phone,

The last landline

That I wouldn't dare utilize

(How presumptuous!)

The click.

The click.

The click.

Men (Swearing, Power Steering, & Me)

I can hear it from my fingers as they slip
Over the screen I clutch with panic.
It will not save me—
I am stuck.
iamstuck.
iamstuck.
I am frozen,
Chosen
Again
By false nicety—
By the light of swollen gods,
That applaud my diminishment.

See what you get for feeling safe?
This.
This.
This.
Lock.
Click.
Hiss.
The breath lets itself out.
I wish it took me too.

Anika Snyder

Young Glove
(Do Not Take the "G" Off)

We settle in
Our copper field,
Our russet slice of lawn.
We shuffle books
And facts between us—
Let knowledge be our pawn.

I take a chance
And smile to see
That you have done the same.
The timid step.
The wayward glance.
The commencement of our game.

I do not deal in fantasy.
I'm much too old for play.
And yet, I feel a Fay-ish warmth
Wind coyly 'round the day.

Men (Swearing, Power Steering, & Me)

I read to you from Rilke,
In the English that I know.
You answer back in German,
In the twilight afterglow.

We dine on Turkish food in town,
Where curbs are far too high.
We need no wheat to fill us up,
My humor is so rye.

You, a kind and softened pink.
Me, a harsher blue.
We each get books
And each rings up
At eighteen sixty-two ($).

Just In Time

He hated everything real about me—
My chaos, my caustic character,
The wetness around my eyes, perennial pools,
The deepening lack of my knowing
As he omitted and evaded more and more.

My concern for his topographic imprint
Was curative to him—
That I worried and wondered.
That I drove myself to distraction.

He needed the banquet of my panic—
To establish his own appetite.
To know how to surrender just enough
So that I'd be kept alive on hope alone
And be allowed to continue my deliverance to him—
Of heart, of body, of self.

To satiate completely—
To be swallowed in felt.
To be soft again after abrasion,
The only kindness he provided.
To chafe me to erosion
And leave me bare to bear his absence.

Men (Swearing, power steering, & me)

Single (Thank God)

My mind and shins are splinted
From the roads that I have sprinted
And conclusions I have jumped to.

I run through streets and feats,
I thought I couldn't pull off—
Like my top in a bed
With a friend of a friend,
Whose desire ends
Where my spirit begins.

I wish I were plastic,
Instead of elastic—
I think it'd feel better to break
Than to bend.

In Even Measures

I feel my individuation
Sprouting from the moss of your derision.
Feel how fractious I become beneath complaint.
I feel with desperate sureness,
My potential took its leave
And is waiting,
Eyes divine,
Beyond this love.

MEN (SWEARING, POWER STEERING, & ME)

WHATEVER I CAN SEE

I point at whatever I can see:
The green tips of fava plants,
The wet sea of rice fields,
The flowering grove of almond trees.

I point at whatever I can see,
And you give me names for the vision.

You catch a red-eared slider by the pond,
Hold it delicately. Show—
The slick illustrious head
Hiding quietly inside itself,
Like song in guitar strings.

You tell me electrifying things:
Transformers, power lines.
We stand above an owl, dead from collision.
We watch like hawks,
Then shake our heads sadly to regain humanity.

We let the world bloom around us.
We see growth in our wandering.
You show me pepper from its tree,
Ground between two fingers.

ANIKA SNYDER

Maple and oak—
Estuaries, marshland.
The way to hold a bottle for a little lamb.
How to make fried pickles—
Extricate stuck cars from snow.

You show me levity,
And my gravity
Falls short.

You show me how loving can feel.
When it's done softly.
And kindly.
And slow.

I point at whatever I can see.
You name the world for me.
I nod and offer little "ohhhhhs,"
Like it is no big deal to have my life expand.

I write you poetry in exchange—
You pat my knee and smile.
And I wonder if it is the same—
You, naming things seen.
Me, naming things felt.
Both of us different for our sharing,
Like a bridge across two banks,
Shuttering to have been anything
But one.

Men (Swearing, Power Steering, & Me)

Beeline

I have looked for all my loves at the bottom of cereal
Boxes. I have flipped the contents upside down and
Shook until grim relief revealed futility in Cheerio
Crumbs and aortic dust.

I have stacked my returns on the counter. I have glared
At the cat—the cat likes to bat at raisin bran because he
Thinks it is bug-like and inviting.

I have worried myself sick
Trying to find my loves.
I have disgorged the pantry of its cashews and dried
Figs—I have littered the liner of my trash can with
Opening lines and lines of opened plastic.
I have fallen down the stairs twice,
Carrying armloads of Triscuits.

I have a sudden fear
That all my loves have curdled
In the milk.

ANIKA SNYDER

To Begin Things (with Feeling)

In the end, it was the shades that did it.
The slight variegation of mold,
A mycology of minute proportions,
The driving force behind the leaving,
A cough—
An allergy to something in the room,
That subsumed
The idea of the person it belonged to.
So that *they* were the allergen,
some human-shaped spore
That bore no significance other than infection.

"What would I gain by living with you?"
Was said.
So too,
"Being with you is a chore."

And the shades, laying patiently—
The mold, euphoric.
Taking hold in such a way,
Lasting longer
Than the people
It abhorred.

MEN (SWEARING, POWER STEERING, & ME)

ON FRAGILE GROUND

I am at my parents' house—
Ukiah, California.
He is at the Grafton Hotel—
Dublin, Ireland.
We are on a break or broken up or in the midst of
getting back together.
I am shattered, sheltered, somber, salacious, salivating
for change and clambering against it.

I have made an egg with sauteed tomatoes for lunch and
chewed on a bit of pumpkin bread.
He has become some somnambulist prodigy,
imbibing decadently on jet lag and lager,
maybe a bit of something stronger, for prosperity.

The last time we talked, he stood fringed by my
doorframe, frozen in my laser beam gaze,
wet tears like fear we forgot to take a headcount on.
He doesnotlovemedoesnotloveme,

No—he cannot be a part of this for longer than he has,
my destructive path, a lightning flash to illuminate the
crescendo of my greed. The moremoremore of needing
him to need me in quite the same way—
How does my ignorance stay behind him on the porch,
just outside my line of sight, without being trained?

Is the jaw so fragile that it dissembles the longest
sentences to syllables?
Just so they can squeeze on through
the short staccato of a no, his answer to my pleading, an
echo of the bleeding I know will ensue.

So much pain in the undoing of something you have
built from frayed canvas and stayed hands—
but no one is culpable. This is just how it is.
Do not blame yourself. Oh, San Andreas, let me in!
Show me your ways! I am afraid I am like you
and this is all my fault.

Men (Swearing, Power Steering, & Me)

Solemn

There is no place for the vitriol,
No outlet for it to lay.
I play with its lightness between my fingers,
Feel the heat of its implied control,
The way I have no room to love now—
To live, free from the confines of a hateful heart.

There is no place for the vitriol, for the rage,
For the raving—
There is the saving of lemon peels to suck on,
To smile through
The bitterness like a test to overcome—
See how strong my taste buds?
See how small my grimace?
Another reminder
That I can withstand you.

I have ransacked my closet,
Gotten rid of your jackets,
Your bracketed words,
The wiles and whimsy,
The flimsy promises you made—
I have recycled my belief in forever
Because I believe in sustainability.

And the pained excuses of retraction—
Detract only from the name (forever)
And not the thing it frames.

I cleaned out my car the other day.
I found the bit of cardboard where you say
I could have my way with you.
The signature and witness—
The litmus of our time together
Shoved under my front seat like an uncouth indictment,
The thing forgotten
Until churned up, panting in a purging.

I left it where it lay,
I let you stay
A little longer.

MEN (SWEARING, POWER STEERING, & ME)

THERE THEY ARE FOLKS

Wednesday walks on unnervingly.
There is a man on a golf course in a gray hat
Drinking a tall can of Coors,
Tucked more tightly to the hillside
Than a fingerless hand.

The man is coming undone,
Spun silk dissected by breath and breeze.
He sees the lump of his life in golf ball sizes—
Alive as the beer in his belly,
Somehow telling more now
About the person he cannot permit himself to be.

In the park, there is a man with a metal detector and
Machete-adjacent knife.
His wife
Is unaware he lost his job
And is looking for coins in curtains of grass
And shades of hope he must bend down to see.

The misery.

The misery.

The pumpkins laughing on the porches—

Lit up at night by frightful curses and cheap candles.

The wicked handle. The squinting—

The luck springing from blue-mooned eyes

And useless crying.

The youth, a dream as—

The gourds guard the door.

The men unmooring.

The handles burning and stinging.

Palms as psalms of absolution.

Nothing true in action anymore.

Just the storm in the distance,

Coming with insistence.

The men on different plains

But plain

To see.

Men (Swearing, Power Steering, & Me)

On His Birthday No Less

I do not like the way he loves me.
Have you heard the rain today? The sky is sobbing!
I do not like the cold constance,
The harsh reproval of my softness—
The grass must be so glad to have a drink!
I do not like his slick dismissals,
Which I swallow to avoid a confrontation.
The dogs all don cute raincoats for their walks!
I do not like the way he loves me.
But what does that matter to the rocks?

The Answer to a Question Posed in Panic

Tremulously, lightly
I forsake you
To try it on, a casual surrender.
It is so much like quitting sugar for a week, a month.
Something impossible until done.
A recrimination from the body,
A craving so desperate for relevance,
For relief
That it lets belief be blind.

You, heart half closed,
Let me find the grip to yank it shut
Completely.
If for nothing else but a panic of desire
To be seen as useful,
Which made me redundant for the
Clinging keen of my trying.
The distasteful availability of uncertain love,
Which professes itself in possessiveness and pugnacity.

Men (Swearing, Power Steering, & Me)

In gripping, in griping.
My mouth slack with need,
Infected with yearning.

I pretend in my mind that you are gone from me.
I let the secret slights be made real.
I condemn your articulation, your cocksure saunter.
I counter your liveliness with silent spates of time,
Minutes of rhinestone insincerity—
The prettiness of my lacking
Finally, a break for you.

I am so much more to you
When I let myself be small,
When I am shadow bound and lurching,
When the searching I allow myself is only in your eyes,
When I let belief be blind.

ANIKA SNYDER

You Make, I'll Mind; It's Up to You

I hope your dreams have cobwebs
That brooms can't sweep.

I hate the way your teeth smile.
I hope they crack against your bad intentions/breath.
And eek out little shrieks of terror—
Make like terriers and bark up every wrong tree,
Chase every bone that sways their way—
The flesh; thick, sweet, tender.

Maybe I will run behind,
Eyes askance, deciding,
Whether to whistle for you.
Or flee.

Men (Swearing, power steering, & Me)

Have You Ever Loved a Porcupine?

In my mind, we are a year over ourselves,
A combined tenacity, simple instructions,
Like love and kindness—
Pliable, only at your discretion.

My hang ups are hang dry only.
No machine can sort me out.
Give me open air and the structure of plastic.
Maybe thin grins, if I get too wrinkled.
Unfurl for me myself.
I've forgotten what I'm made of.

Anika Snyder

Not on Christmas Eve

The stalking,
Hung.
Police tape across
The left side of
The street.

Pursuit was short.
I'm lucky;
I was faster on my feet.

MEN (SWEARING, POWER STEERING, & ME)

CALLING A FRIEND,
THE TIMES TABLE OF UNSTABLE THINGS

I press my fat palm against my flaming lips—
Sandpaper
Igniting.

The heady expansionism of the words I cannot say—
The territory,
Your awareness.
My intention seeping through,
Like mist over low fields.

As such, the flammable nature of my mind
Begs kind thoughts to soothe the turmoil,
The rigorous policing to ensure
That no one is burned by my chatter.
What does it matter?
My thoughts have nuance you cannot believe.

Like how I am not the sieve you need,
The vessel to pour
Your own good estimation of yourself—
Into pulp free orange juice,
Into weak bottles of wine,
Like how I am not your therapist.
Not your mother.
Not your thing to control.
Like how I am just a woman,
Just a skeptical person—
Just a girl.

But the nuance is full of words and spikes and vines
You do not understand.
So, I will let them be silent,
Until they are wrapped so tightly around you
That you cannot wriggle free
When I scream.

MEN (SWEARING, POWER STEERING, & ME)

TO EDITORIALIZE

The creepy crawlers are out.
The night adjacent dawn
Yawns.
In unruly ululations,
I am sure my feet will greet their forms—
The squirm of squid-like bodies in the dark,
The kickoff of disgusting things:
I soar above the meters.

Meted by licentious men
That measure my worth in frothy ways,
Like my unrelenting gaze,
Or the way I shift
Beneath their own.

The tone,
A somber agitator
When turned high enough to hear.
My body.
My fear.
Their choice,
They say.
Like there is no other way
But violence.

ANIKA SNYDER

The Men I Met Today

I have my black turtleneck on—
Some rings,
Necklace,
Like luck at my throat.
Cold and nominal,
The furrowing of sexuality,
Small beneath my smile.

I read my book between sips of coffee, sopping
Warmly through my body.
There is a man who wants to take my picture with his
Film camera.
I disappear into his lens—
Transported into physical memory,
Into figurative fame
Who's frame may one day curl into decay.

A boy with a joint behind his ear
Asks me for my number.
I do not fear the forest
When I have been filled with trees.
I make no move to cut the wood
That needs no sap to stick to—
I am free,
Like wild things before they're caught and killed.

Men (Swearing, Power Steering, & Me)

So, I say no
In a soft appeal
To be released,
Before my skin
Is torn to bits.
To be let go,
Before his anger hits.

A man,
Stooped low with lumbar spondylosis,
Gives me a box of incense because he likes my hair.
I think it only fair
I set the curls on fire.
At least the embers
Would perfume the air.
What would I care
For censer?
When the essence of consumption
Censors the evidence of my use,
Until the only unredacted lines
Are how I appear to you.

Holding For Nothing

Today is the 7th Annual Acknowledgment
Of your betrayal.
The hepatic insurance,
Girding the lemon melancholy of a drop in the hat,
A distinguished drink on the brink of metamorphosis—
Get a load of this:
The potation I think I've found a use for,
The mourning you introduced to night
To make the sadness paler than the moon.
You cannot swoon for love
When you're fighting phases unrelated—
When the gibbous is guileless,
When the crescent, crescendoing catharsis
 Leaves you flat out with its feeling.

Today is the 7th Annual Acknowledgement
Of your betrayal.
I am not used to broken things beyond me.
(Plates and hearts.)

Men (Swearing, Power Steering, & Me)

Ceramic matter that shatters
Into pieces unreliably rent.
The begging
In the small shard
Lost behind the couch.
To be found
And returned to wholeness—
The begging
In the fragment
Lost behind your leaving
Of me
That yearns for your restoration.

Anika Snyder

Wool Makes for Itchy Eye Masks

A little sore after
Old injuries—
Come cautiously.

Whatever happened to second guesses?
Shouldn't we be having them by now?
The wool, sheep shorn, over eyes that will not stray—
A herding nightmare
If the pasture is overeaten and bare.

No dog can prepare the way out.
Silently, we wait for hunger
To move the lambs legs,
The drum, a thunder
Of insistence at their necks.
The canine's canines,
A marvelous map on naked skin—
The thinning of relief,
The flock freezing in the field,
The witnessing,
An editing on what we believed.

A little sore after—
The eyes, a dull itch, from what's been pulled over.

MEN (SWEARING, POWER STEERING, & ME)

THE ANGRY MAN

I have let an angry man inside me.
The grief
Cracks
Beneath my ribs,
An open furnace.

I cannot stand in line
At the grocery store
With a fire
So immense,
Spitting in my organs.

I have forgone
The places
I used to find joy.

I worry I will burn the world
With my steady drift of flame.
And I am to blame
Because I have let an angry man
Inside me.

ANIKA SNYDER

As if He Didn't Know

And you slip slightly—
Catch yourself in the corner of my eye.

The putrescent pleurisy of your remark
Wedges in against my lungs.
I hack.
You demure,
Hand on the tissue box.

"What's wrong?"
You say

My eyes are saucers.

Death, No Designer

There is no earthbound place
Where the angels descend.
There are only—
Litanies of lies
That lay lacelike
Over the latticework of self.

The ego depressed—
Like the outline
On sheets
That reek
Of mutualistic mutilation.
The cadaver kiss
Of stony lips
Against pleas
Of reconciliation.

And now,
Your eyes are colder by degrees—
I seize up beneath their frost.

Just Saying!

He was a very good talker
Because he didn't do it much.
His lips were pierced
With the subtle understanding of redundancy.
I made do with what I had
(a bigger brain)
That my refrain
Kept falling down in front of.

He was a very good walker
Because he kept getting DUIs.
At least his lies
Were sobering.

Men (swearing, power steering, & me)

Linger and Lose

We meet
Like peace after chaos,
Under a sky revealing stars shyly—
As if it is not quite sure
It can pull them off.

Our words are cobblestone steps
We press bare feet against.
Some have been waiting all day in the sun,
And so, we blister. The sum—
Of our hurts
A way around loneliness,
To be understood
In desperation
Is to be known.
To survive.

I need you now,
With painful clarity.
But I let my arms fall,
Discarded wind from empty gestures.
I ask you to go—
And you know me
And refuse.

But I am convincing
And poorly lit in twilight.
So, you let me push you into the abyss of singularity
And leave.

I linger and lose just one more minute—
The injustice of the loss will strike me later
When I am alone.
I wonder,
If you saw my grimace grow,
To follow you down the street.

MEN (SWEARING, POWER STEERING, & ME)

JORTS AND SANDALS

I need to stay fashion forward.
So, I wear your face some days.
I'm sorry—
I tasked my mother with my outreach,
And she beseeched me
(one whimper, one whisper)
To be true to myself.

When I was three days old,
A doctor made a face when I cried.
I decided then, to be so stoic
No egoic
Man could phase me.
This, of course,
Has not worked.
So, I borrow faces
To receive the graces
Normal people unironically enjoy.

Anika Snyder

We Fought 14 Times Today

We are wires cut
Along the length of our ulnas—
We jump apart when they collide.

Just last week,
We were
Two halves of a book.

Our bones,
the heinous spine,
That separates art.

But now,
We are live wires.
So, give water a wide berth,
Which makes sailing impossible—
Smooth or otherwise.

MEN (SWEARING, POWER STEERING, & ME)

OF ALL TRADES

I have been thinking lately
About the patterns I repeat for you—
Zoo animal locked,
Tightly sprung in pastoral rungs
Of lengthening ladders—
The fatter the grief grows, the slower I climb—
I mind very little
But for the small, sweet memory of you
Gouged in the back of my eyes.

The tantalizing breach
Of many lidded emotional reallocation.
Like, can I rip the roots from our love
And take it to different climates?
I find it in the pockets of my vests,
The vast elicit baseness of its refusal to desert.
I am stuck on you forever,
Thinking, blankly,
That this is what I must deserve.

Anika Snyder

The Briefest Exchange

Muscles tied to flagpoles of steady bones—
The tones; winnowing, winnowing.
Minnows
Burrowing
In schools we cannot learn from,
Groupings of imaginings
Set straight in retrospect.

There is claim in your silence
That I find solace in.
Your refusal to know me,
A guarantee
I can sauté with my broccoli—
How sweet the consumption of truth,
When it is cruel and base.

Men (Swearing, Power Steering, & Me)

How sustaining,
Without the doubt of further straying.
With the knowing
That what is achievable
Is wanting,
And what I can dream for
Is blissful
In conscious consideration.
A prize of overactive imagination—
Your kindness,
A heaven,
At last.

Anika Snyder

Glow-in-The-Dark Bracelets Upstage the Unfaithful

Fools that we are—
We become
Rare and blushing past 5 p.m.
The stars rushing past our egos,
Tripping on the long, low-matted tail
Of our wanting.

Fools that we are—
Something
In the rafters
Of the world we revisit
Will not let us leave
The building
Without cursing us.

Men (Swearing, Power Steering, & Me)

The sidewalks, coming up with new rifts
To catch our dragging toes.
The night,
Making holes of its matter
To lose ourselves within,
Just until the thin yield
Of morning light
Pronounces itself brackish
On the back of a hand you raise
To brush the hair from my eyes.

In the room, alone,
I wait beneath sheets gone cold and hostile.
Fools that we are—
In those few minutes before you return,
I know it is just me that is foolish.
Arriving again at the idea of a warmth
That dies beside brighter things—
Like the sun
Or the other one
That you love.

Nature Break

The nature breaks are meant to provide a little respite from the heavy poems. They are an ode to the wonders of the natural world. My work has brought me ample opportunity for retrospective instruction, carried out by witnessing the delightful way the earth works. I find myself so frequently inspired by the simplicity of the outdoors and deeply indebted to the feeling of expansiveness it provides me.

Briars

NeeduponNeeduponNeeduponNeed.
Empty as—
The field behind the fire station.
Cordoned off in traffic cone spires, the desire ...
Gone out of the grass to burn.
No more,
It says.
It has been prescribed too much; the land begs off—
Complains of a stomachache,
Toothache—
Anything
To have the mutilation end.

No exhaustive excuses—
The intended uses ...
It is aimed at good!
To learn!
To live!
To laugh!
(To lose.)
Too much has been taken.
Higher purpose makes even
Pious heads spin.
Lay low, Earth.
Bend one more time,
Again.

Nature break

Fall and Then Recover

Fall vignettes.
Persimmon saplings strapped to lattices.
Dark, wet bark of redwoods.
Grove growing giants,
Green with gratitude for
The rain.

Shoes, damp.
Socks, gritty against gravel stowing away in size eight
Keens.
Keening soul searching for
Forensic evidence of happiness.
In the gray sky.
Laughter dies
And is reborn.

Fall vignettes.

Pit bulls in raincoats.

Saturday sleep rubbed from the eyes of Protestants.

Work ethic

Lost

To car shows driving by

And cow choirs—

Singing hymns into the mist.

I consider this

The essence of being,

The being of essence,

Essential in existential terms.

I consider—

The moments I codify

And decide, in two breaths and one thought,

To un-name my experiences

And simply be.

Nature break

Wintertime Glee

The cold inches along my skin.
I measure my breath against its biting chill,
Focus on the bracing relief of foot warmers
　Tucked hastily into hiking boots.

Roots air themselves out on cliff sides—
　Showing off their natural erosion,
　Like a child with new shoes,
　Before a full day of school,
　Has tarnished them.

I hem myself in,
Sew peace to the length of me.
Feast on the day,
Like a woman starved—
Until its beauty is inside of me,
Deeper than the frost.

Lemon Tree

Under the lemon tree—
Planks support
The weight of some world
I cannot see.
The awning, leafy canopy—
The July air,
Thinner, frail
With arm between the thorns.
 I am upheld.

A vein to find the courage
To ravage.
See: lemon tree.
See: sour.
See: me beneath the power—
Of someone else, again.

My bargain chip,
One fruit, one smile.
Please be pretty—
A sweet we know nothing of—
Please,
Flower kindly
Before
Dissection.

Nature Break

Bleed out profound guesses.
Soil the soil
With the riches
Of my poor soul.
Leave me with you—
Lemon tree, true.
The wavering is something I've left up to chance.
But be bold ... as I have yet to be.

Leave me with you!
With the world I cannot see—
The thorns.
The canopy.
The wild you drop in yellow prototypes.
The creation and care.
The fair effort of extinction.
To have lived as you—
Let me do so.
Set me free.

ANIKA SNYDER

The Things I Bring to Life

There's a snake at the old barn door again.
She has returned the past few days,
Like a living ink stain.
Resurrected by cosmic pull—
The full measure of the world,
A slipping mirage beneath her scales.

The heat, a pressing hand,
Commanding her back inside—
The sleek concrete, a vestibular heaven
Containing coolness, caution, calamity.
Rich, patterned seams break at her slithering,
Bow, fevering.

I do not care what she wants—
I want her gone.
She has slid off my arm and fallen before me.
She is pleading with me!
She is seething…

Nature Break

"What?" I whine.

I cannot hear the things she admits or omits

Because I close my ears to her screaming.

The ranch staff remove her.

They are afraid, like I am.

I keep my armband tight against my healing skin—

Three days ago, I got a tattoo of her sister.

She must miss her.

I just wish she'd let me be.

Flies

The line snags
A hundred mouths
But lets them go.
You slide
Down hills
On rolling ankles,
Soft dry grass for youthful feet,
The meeting of the water
Against your ego.
You need,
Just one fish
Before you leave.

NATURE BREAK

DRAGGING LINES

There is no mammoth sentinel at the end of the world.
There is a vista and a house—
A deserted basketball hoop, gamely watchful.
A wooden fence forgiven by wind for having stood too
Long against it.

There is a mist that rolls in, tagging tree line,
A breath and a sorry restraint.
The lake on standby,
Rod-straight limbs at attention above moss forests,
Desire frugal rocks.

There is the husk of a buoy—orange.
A dog—copper.
A book—half-read.

Where the mark goes, you go.
How has half a story elapsed?
The hollow log, a faulted system,
Carries you, overwrought—
The weight
Of everything you could have been.
A bend
In decision.
Once so simply understood—
Now settled in like luxury,
Or a softly spoken prayer.
A relief to be moved—
Without going anywhere.

Drinking (oops, I did it again!)

Have you ever felt at the top of the world at the bottom of a bottle? The larger the lager, the later the emotional pain. It might be kicking the can down the road but at least syllable soccer is sustained.

Telekinesis

I am small and sad and
Wooden.
Dry leaves and matches
Make me quiver.
My liver
Bares its shroud
In proud disfigurement.
Little flags flown white
Across interior Me.
My cabinet,
My constituency
Has no consistency.
I am disinherited from reason.
I fear
My season
Is at its close.

Drinking (Oops, I did it again!)

Whatever Comes

Whatever comes, comes with fury.
I leave my mouth open, to catch the blurry
Entrails of old beliefs and brief delusions.
I am sick with the poison I partook in
With glee.
"I am me!"
I shout
Until I forget
How to be.

Hi Dottie

I get real sad.
I get real stiff.
I get real drunk to deal with it.
When I get sloshed
And slip away,
I can endure another day!

Drinking (Oops, I Did It Again!)

Not, As You Were

I have pinprick eyes
And pointed teeth.
I am not unkind,
But I am not sweet.

I am fearsome, deadly, droll, and dross—
I am almost always at a loss.
Whenever I incur some wrath,
I draw myself a bubble bath.

I find life lacking,
Sick, and dull.
But hey,
At least my glass is full.

Anika Snyder

What I See, Visionary Gain

Mud impression—
Two horseshoes, overlain.
An infinity.
An eternity.
I squelch the tips of my toes into the forever—
It comes halfway loose,
Losing its nerve.
I plotter—
Plot my route,
Route my plot
Amongst the headstones.
Mine (does not play well with others).
The serifs sing.
The angels clutch their purls.
I knit my brows—this the yarn I weave.
In-out-in-out—
The forever,
The interim of never.

Drinking (Oops, I did it again!)

I wait empty-handed.

Hand empty gestures to the clouds—

The nimbus numbskulls mistake it for prayer,

That rare, inalterable affliction of the hopeful.

(I believe in dead dignities who perished for my sins.)

Lie innocence lie.

Stay still, lest coagulated blood leads

Damnation to your side.

The sightless hands of DNA provide

Addiction/benediction

In the wisdom of the strands.

In nature,

This nurtured indolence burns me through.

Why waste my days for that which does not serve me?

When it's me I over serve ...

My Bible: the bottle.

My sin: an omission.

My toenails are dirt filled,

Hoof cloven, contrition.

ANIKA SNYDER

Parenthetical

I'm sure you know by now,
The parenthetical nature of my affliction,
The underlying implication of its heft—
A shadow beneath the weight of my normalcy.

Perhaps you suppose
I have been cured of my disease,
And I now enjoy the benefits of stability and sanity.

Perhaps you suppose
In that same strain
That pigs can fly.

I cannot imagine your surprise
When, upon leaving me,
you found the world an open and honest place.

Drinking (Oops, I did it again!)

And that the hearth of my arms
Was a ring of hell, which you had so cleverly escaped.
I do applaud your egress!
I am impressed, even ...
That you made off with as much of yourself as you did.

I wonder if you linger upon me still,
If your mind disobeys your healing heart
And you consider me.

Does my intellect flash like brazen lightning
Across your tormented skies?
The lies it fabricated,
The voice it assumed in argumentative aplomb.

Do my arched brows pull the corners of your lips
When you drink in their memory?
It is of little or no consequence.
For we are horribly, irrevocably, finished.

We are two banks admitted to guarding
Either side of a pond—
Forcibly separate,
Dangerously close,
If not for a substance other than ourselves,
Lying in wait between.

And how fitting an analogy—
The wet slick of potable liquid,
That unbridgeable fairway.
(What's the fair way to put this?)
ONE of us has a problem with drink.

DRINKING (OOPS, I DID IT AGAIN!)

AT 3:02 AM

Maybe you don't have to touch wet bark
To feel the branching off of self.
Those separate parts that fit the whole of soul,
Within the joining of their joints.

Maybe it was not self but sister
That splintered from the tree we came from.
The knots along our limbs—
The grim facsimile of growth.

Maybe we toed the line behind towed cars
Outside closed bars
And forgot the smell of rainwater
And snail slime on agapanthus leaves.

Maybe we—
Me as self,
Me as sister,
Sidestepped feeling because we thought
We ought to hold onto what was felt.

Not knowing—
Because no one told us
You don't have to touch wet bark
To feel the branching off of self.

ANIKA SNYDER

Blues and Cocktails

Brass and barn, wood somehow old and new.
Arm around shoulder—
Hand cradling head.
Gentle.
Ice in warm grip—
Something so slippery in the way it moves.

Almost out of reach—
Teachable.
Tautology only
In digits without substitution.
An always in the fingernails—
Numinous, stretching.
All encompassing, warm.

Blues in cuticles
Dance across hairline.
A sister surliness
In snappish possessiveness—

Drinking (Oops, I did it again!)

The impish supposition of ownership,
Believable in percentages,
Like cocktails and wine—
Whiskey, neat.

How clean the presentation: To be loved.
The bar so low,
Even fleas can grab a drink
And stay awhile.

Death and the Maiden

In green glass, the spark of hot liquid,
A courage divulged slowly, the pools of false light—
Over pool tables,
Hands in the shallows,
Floating softly out of sight.

The golden carbonation,
The taxation of imbibed melancholy.
Calling again, the god I once knew.
The ex on the phone,
Drawn now, into some new drama.
The line ringing and ringing—
The ears, too.

The sound of distant emptiness,
A resounding understanding—
He is gone.
The green glasses on the shelf.
The men behind the bar.
The car outside.
Pointing to home.

Drinking (Oops, I did it again!)

Some Say November

To return to ground hollowed by embarrassment,
Bravery somehow
Softened, often with alcohol
And the chiding of communal humanity.
The forgiveness, the understanding,
Tiled expertly around the eyes.
An antechamber of monumental proportions—
The torsion of heart,
Like a hiccupping beneath floorboards,
A promise to remember
The press of time.
How dying is an accented word
When spoken on living tongues.
The gravity,
The cavity
Of understanding will fill
Just once
Before you go.

At The Bottom There Are Rocks

Not for nothing—
If.
Is there a god—
When.
My hand cannot—
Hold itself up any longer.
When.
The stiffness is, for itself, a debasement.

How can I drink the world dry
And leave so much behind?
Not even trying
To disguise
My wanting.

Or ...

The way I hit bar floors—
And lay
With stars for eyes,
Until I am the scene
Of my own decay.

Drinking (Oops, I did it again!)

Justin Trudeau

I am in my prime, minister.
Do not look at my liver.
Look at my eyes.
I think I have a few months left of clarity.

I am in my prime, minister.
I can still run and dance and laugh
Like no one's watching.
I can stick my finger into toasters and grab the
incoherent remnants of my breakfast—
Risk the burning like I'm turning into heat itself.

I can become
The things that hurt me,
Instead of having them destroy me.
I am lucky to be one with my undoing—
Like a zipper
Consumed by its teeth,
Leaving cavities of space
For new things to fill—
Ideas,
Bills,
Desirability (only in extremes).

Anika Snyder

It seems unkind of me, minister—
To be so good at the bad things
And take the people that I love
With me.

DRINKING (OOPS, I DID IT AGAIN!)

U-TOWN

Hometown.
Cherries de-pitted,
Gouged of essence—
Exploded eulogies of a once cohesive sweetness,
No longer.

Hometown.
If Homer had his Odyssey,
Let me have my oddity.
The mythology of my strangeness,
Confirmed in chance encounters
That somehow get profounder
The more people
That you tell.

Hometown.
The local bar
Has a hold of my grey matter.
I think that they'd be sadder
If this novel doesn't sell.

ANIKA SNYDER

At the End, You'll Find Yourself

In the bracing dark
The night ascends,
Wings itself
To grace.

The hands aligned
In knuckled prayer,
The soft and fair advancement—
A minute pulling back of what is real,
Like teeth
In grimacing structure.

The tutored tailing of understanding,
Chasing meaning in gray hair and motel rooms.
In the dark, wartime almost—
The gunning for
Surrender.

The turrets of the castle,
Your mind—
Enshrined, at last,
In alcoholic motes
You will not deign to cross.

Drinking (Oops, I did it again!)

It is Five AM Somewhere

It is 5:00 a.m. somewhere.
Here, it is 5:00 p.m.
So, I slice
My finger on
The cheese knife and drink a bottle of wine.

It is 5:00 a.m. somewhere.
They would be appalled at the whole
Geriatric mess of my mistakes:
The same old ones, again.

It is 5:00 a.m. somewhere.
A man named Paul is
Probably taking a walk
With his deleterious pandering.
Pondering the way his ex-wife left three years ago.

Paul, I too, am stuck—
Broken open.
So, I drink the way they used to in the olden days.

The one good thing for me, Paul,
Is that it is 5:00 p.m.,
And I can suck on substance
Until I am cracked in little rifts
That let the tiniest bit of starlight
Peek through.

The Foxhole, the Atheist, Mathematic Conversion:

This is the section for the religiously cynical or searching. I've found myself lurching from belief to belief, like I'm walking on stars, drawing constellations of conclusions. If you take anything from this, make sure that they're all questions.

Christ (Forgive Me)

Entreaties unto dark plastic.
The priest swears the bloodstains are new.
The flowers wet, thick relief in thin petals.
A diagram of disrepair—
The holy Host Ghosts gloatingly through opera houses.
Which stems from which?
The green chlorophyll leviathans—
The departed specters.
The godliest of dogs reversed backwards and revered.
Heavy is the head that wears the crown,
And his head sags.
(The lowliest bloodhound, ears kissing earthworms.)
Out walking my own god, I ran into Jesus disciples.
The one in the peach, flowered dress
Addressed me directly—directed me to a web
I could cite in my soul search.
I politely declined.
Her lips looked so soft.

Death of gods: Deicide Discovery

I have been fearful
That my fingers
Are too close to the throat—
Of all my ideals, my gods.
The icons, the gilding,
The freshwater forests.
Reveal me in plenty.
Review me in pleasure.
The tongues of my yearnings
Have forks to feed sin to.
The tines, the red burning,
Until you are seared through.
My deicide decides
The world's composition.
I have murdered my gods.
I bow down in contrition.

To Rely On Faith

Rattle entombed in trailer tracks—
Metal grating hesitant grins from cracked concrete.
Heat blistered from the earth's core,
Hot suggestions to move on.
Advice geometric on geographic tongues,
Unwelcome, unwanted—
Breaking cows hooves for bovine Bibles
That bind you, unholy, to untrodden pasture.

A voice in a small box.
A button unpressed, the rest we postulate and pose.
Who knows what words to say better
Than an unwitnessed speaker.
The investment, a hope,
Despite a lack of visual aid.
The Savior, a curtain-pull away.

Breakfast At Least, Before Consideration Of Universal Desertion (God)

"I am going to save you,"
It says.
"The gods,"
 It says.
Ah, collegiate pantheon—
Still learning to trust my failings,
My flaws.

The leeches miss my sense of self,
So let me bleed.
Blood let me see—
Beyond this place.
Oh, please believe
Me worthy now …

It says,
"The gods, the gods
  Omniscient few.
  Reward me now
  That I am new.
  I've set myself
  A path to walk.
  Correct my feet.
  Destroy the rocks."

The gods, the gods,
No rhyme to maim.
The broken places verse can sail—
A mast amassed a wind to move.
So, you can too,
With proper breath.

Breathe in
And Out
And in again.
Save yourself, a thing unbent.
Look up!

The Foxhole, The Atheist, Mathematic Conversions

I beg you—
See the hole?
Don't you see the sky is empty?
Your screams are heard and answered
By eagles alone.

Don't you see the clouds are lonely?
Do you think the world would perish in such a way
With help waiting?
Watching?
Until you have just enough merit.

Don't you see you are below the caliber,
When the night recognizes you as starlight
And lifts you to the moon?
Don't you realize there is no beyond,
Except the void,
The veil, that separates me and you?

Adjudicated

What happens but a prolapse of human sentiment?
Legal to the bones.
A signatories fever dream—
This bond.
The filament,
Unraveled at its core.
The closer you inspect
The more things seem to fray.

Soup cans in grocery aisles—
Islands of their own.
Minestrone coastlines
Forecast tsunamis.
Synonymous with gold,
The alchemy of danger.
Boldly proclaimed,
The eternal endeavor.

The Foxhole, the Atheist, Mathematic Conversions

To find reason for disaster
In inflated things,
Like belief or home goods,
Like your cabinet and ours.

The shape of democracy,
Flagrantly recurved.
Folding, shirt sleeves tucked
Into a regret that gets four years to grow.
The prolapse in the lobe,
Temporal at best—
Secular if you let your spirit go.

By Accident

The echo there, all along,
Trapped in tin, reverberating unkindly.
Cover ears covertly.
Schubert transmitting through plumbing—
The pipes breaking, creaking unfairly.
Burst now,
To subsume.
Appendix of unread books—
The book endings
That hold nothing up
But you.

As the car horn blares outside
The time—
Refracted in the tires,
Tired of treading too lightly
Around concepts too concrete to qualify.
The meditative quality
Of knowing nothing.

The back of god's hand,
Revealing a reflection
You try not to believe.

Homecoming

Salmon clouds propound harps and celestial rays—
Warmth like promises kissing trees on tired foreheads.
Awake and be great now.
Embrace innocence.
No Andes but the mountains—
Still bright and bold,
The hills, looking up,
Dressed in the silk of another day—
A chance again,
To remake life.

The bullet trailer,
A "For Sale" sign slung on its meticulous body.
Watching.
Waiting.
The cats—
Beneath its tires,
Ironing concrete
To dispel cracks they dip their nails in.

I am two, four, six times the size I was yesterday—
I park my car and almost slam into the mailbox.
How shoddy the work of time,
To allow me to grow
Without having a place to put me.

Anika Snyder

How I Know I'm Made for Pain

Indecorous, God.

To have given me taste buds

And offered me nectar—

My tongue has expanded in its pleasure, sought—

The tough, tawny bark of softer sweets.

The mark,

Insoluble in water.

The searching,

Dark, without your light to guide me.

Indecorous, God.

To have given me oceans

And taught me to swim—

My arms have grown tired of their reeling.

The feeling,

Going out with the tide.

The meaning, insistent,

Debriding my diving.

The Foxhole, The Atheist, Mathematic Conversions

The bottom,
Come up with its large nose pressed
To my ankles.
Achilles—
The healing
I never achieve.

Relieve me, now.
Believe the sentiment of release—
Know this is the piece
I lacked the knowledge of.
How the sweetness, the loving, can be too neat—
The oceans, the striving, can have you beat.
The effort of trying,
Too futile.

Anika Snyder

I Am Given Tasks, Don't Ask Me How

Today, the hills are evangelical.
They hum a hymn for every heavy heart
That lives below them.
The threat of their prayerfulness is playfulness to me—
They do not know I want to die.
So, I smile,
Like a stretched-out shirt,
Lifted above a head full of catharsis.

Today, in the wake of my suicidality,
I consider getting a sports car.
I want to go fast to my end,
One brilliantly measured stride at a time.
The wheels of misfortune—
A bad pull from a karmic deck,
The debt of which I dog-ear,
Like a page to keep a favorite line.

The Foxhole, the Atheist, Mathematic Conversions

Today, the cold chill in the air
Is a virtuous virgin,
Verging on volunteering.
It lifts its unerring hand to my cheek
And tells me to keep
Breathing.

How kind the veneration
To keep me at my word,
To try and push me into living,
Even though I want to die.
The hills,
The air fighting now,
A battle they know they can't win
But how valiant the effort—
To try.

Nature Break

The nature breaks are meant to provide a little respite from the heavy poems. They are an ode to the wonders of the natural world. My work has brought me ample opportunity for retrospective instruction, carried out by witnessing the delightful way the earth works. I find myself so frequently inspired by the simplicity of the outdoors and deeply indebted to the feeling of expansiveness it provides me.

Zephyr

We walk an even pace, my dog and I.
There is a dead thing in the road
That we both lift our noses to—
She: discerning.
Me: concerning
Myself with death and its formidable inscrutability.

The rain has cleared.
My skin is frail with its cleansing.
I feel the use of my body like fabric for washing—
A thing wrung out until the freshness of youth
Is a small gleeful memory,
Like mirage
In thirsty eyes.

The hills are greening, growing.
I press my palm against my mouth
To keep a cry of grief inside—
The healing the earth provides,
So horribly attainable,
So out of reach
For me.

Nature break

My toes, in their rain boots—
Squeeze against rocks
That stick up like soldiers
Amid the morning dew,
Those solid few sharp-ended stones
That sting and laugh as I am slowing.

The world is singing me out,
And I am going.
My dog and I—
Even paces
But slowing.

ANIKA SNYDER

Hung and Out

With the help of the stars and some light words,
Your face reveals itself to me.
In the glow, the soft shining, I see—
The tender places that you cannot keep hidden.
The dark spilling,
Like a secret prayer,
To cover crow's feet and frown lines alike.
No alien judgment
Or indictment
In the consideration of you.

Just the blue ambiance,
The deepest mark of tomorrow's coming—
The future we put our hands against
Like one giant ball
We hope to stall
A little longer,
Only if just
To catch our tired breath.

In this night,
In our longing,
The screech owls perform an opera.
We will never be as high as they are,
Or as wild.
But we witness
And smile
Because our living bumps against theirs—
So sweetly.

NATURE BREAK

On The Lawn Chairs There are Ants

On the lawn chairs there are ants.
I have left a crumb from some dumb loaf of bread
In hopes they break it with me.

The ants on the lawn chairs are fair figures
In pre-dawn light—
I let them do the New York Times mini crossword,
And they butcher five across.

On the lawn chairs, where the ants romance,
I set up a kissing booth made of the tooth I lost
Last Friday in a bar fight.

The ants on the lawn chairs are all uncles.
I try very hard to explain to my dog,
But he gets stuck on the letter "u"
That has been left in destitution.

On the lawn chairs there are ants,
And I am on the ground.
I have found no station better
To observe the life around me.
I hope my softness lets them know
I stake my life on little things like them.
I hope they don't condemn me for my loving.

ANIKA SNYDER

IMAGINE MY SURPRISE

The barn is quiet in the low light of
A fair November evening.
The long fingers of sunset wrap around wooden beams
And the seams of small smiles
Pressed hopefully to the soft forelocks of stalled horses.

The brush of twilight
Promises the raw delight
Of peaceful passage home
On country roads
That stretch
Far outside
The reach of high beams and high hopes.

I journeyed so long
To feel the song of my soul—
No new goal would suffice.
I was ice on rinks that reeked of dull blades and
Thunder-threatened skies—
There was always something on the horizon.

Nature Break

I grew brazen in the wake of predicted upheaval.
I unraveled the world in uneven ways
So that the weight weighed me down uncomfortably.
But that is done now.

And I wait for the dawn,
The same way
The low light waits for me—
Expectantly, lovingly, hushed.

To Run

I exist in the sprint,
In the arms held back.
Wind befriending bloated muscles—
A heckling high that rushes in on running shoes
softened by unforgiving pavement and negligent rocks.

I exist in the lung, devoid of air—
Until it rushes back in jagged snatches,
The mitt held against oxygen
To catch just one more breath.

I exist in the soaring—
In legs stretched above land in eternal, ecstatic leaps,
The boundlessness of flight
When flight feels far from fantasy.

I exist in my body—
Finally, finally.
I can feel my fingernails, my shins.
I can feel the center of me
That I somehow keep losing
When I walk around bends.

NATURE BREAK

THE WAY THE NIGHT IS

The way the night is—
The supple supply of its sustenance.
The cool mooring of the morning
When it finds its way home.
The incense intense on the milder things,
Like the rims of water glasses
And suggestions of casual surrendering.

Tomorrow comes wandering on weary feet,
Curious and sweet but naive in its gentleness.
Knowing comes at the cost of yesterday,
The way things have always been—
The superstition in the wood knotted
With knocks and wishes to stave off fate,
The shape of hope,
A sunshiny moon refracting starlight—
The amalgamation of natural things in unnatural order.
To coalesce, in tight-lipped wonder.
To sunder the life we led before,
And sew it up—new.

I have leased a little night now,
Still slipping on its silk.
Regaining my footing,
Windmilling my arms,
Watching for puddles in the deepening dark—
Aware of the stark endings of me.
The car horns and birdsong,
The light of the leaves on inquisitive breezes,
The way I am whole without trying to be.
Finding myself again,
Once the light rests its eyes.
Becoming and growing.
In night.
In time.

The Sky is Moved to Tears

It caught in me,
In rhythmic ripples,
A glassy kind of certitude—
A peacefulness,
A plaintiveness,
A heart dispatched of turpitude.

It moved me to unceasing joy—
The water ringed and self-contained.
I hoped I'd not be at the pond
To see the calm dispelled with rain.

Death (this is all just conjecture)

And taxes, more like. But the scythes are hooked around our middles, and I suppose my consideration of it is just really good prep work.

ANIKA SNYDER

THE C WORD

The space beside my head needs filling.
So, I swivel—swing—oscillate.
My dimensionless mind
Does unmentionable things
To voids.

My father, my progenitor,
Is pronounced cancerous by the lab and a doctor.
They have space beside their heads.
They hold them steady.

I am sympathetic to clocks today,
The way they swivel—swing—oscillate,
The way they are ALWAYS late
(and on time and early).
It must be so hard
To be so many things
At once.

Death (This is all just conjecture)

The Things They Don't Tell You In Middle School

She was very grand, the medium.
The misnomer blinked, unseemly.

She was divine in her crystals,
Which helped her divine the date of my death—
(Undisclosed) and my life (in repose).

She told me, her voice velveteen with surety,
That in this life I will not meet my soulmate.
I shrugged farther than my shoulders could stomach.

Tore a ligament in my neck
And sagged a little lower in my seat—
"No matter," I said in a river of words so intense
She wrung her hair of its wetness.

"No matter," I repeated.
Let us move on.

She told me I have been a woman
In thirteen lives already.

I shook in my womanly boots.
Fourteen times the fairer sex,
I guessed she meant to say.

I did not dare whisper an inquiry
About the part of me that does not feel
As much on quiet days.

My mother, said she.
Has lived seven lives with me.
(This the eighth.)

We have been mother-daughter,
Daughter-mother—
In one, sister-sister.

My twin and I, she whispered,
Have been twins in every life we've shared.
Threetimesover—
Twins!
Twins!
Twins … again in present.

The crystals—
Angelic torrents to tear through trauma,
Watched as silent sentinels tried,
In geode good humor, to find my pain.

Death (This is all just conjecture)

Instead, perceived my shame shrunk
(Somewhere near my bladder)—
My UTI machine.
They cleared it out!

My body cleaned—
The sugar in my skin broke an even sheen
Across its surface—
I was shining for the world to see.

"More," I uttered.
"More," I urged.
"More," I spluttered, until she disclosed
My credit (Poor) and karma (Good).

I asked after books.
She said I contained them.
I asked after loves.
She said I detained them.

She touched my forehead with her eyes
And told me trust was just my cross to bear—
My lack of it—no guts, sans trust.
We all have things we cannot share.

She saw my life spill like coffee from a jaunty mug.
Forget tea leaves.

The yellow brown of my years stained a map
Only she could discern.
I was puddlesick—
My stomach groaned at being known.

Thus, I was seen.
I was told of my own agency—
"YOU CAN CHOOSE," said she.
She said, "You have choice!"

I lamented.
I was hot with it—
The choice.

I can choose!
I am destined only to die.
This much ...
This much I cannot do.

Death (This is all just conjecture)

Were We Here Before?

I live in shade.
I swallow shadow.
I am a thing you ring in dark.
My body sings.
My heart is hallowed.
On the ground, I leave my mark.
When, in future, I am buried,
I hope the worms will love my bones
And sustain themselves with marrow.
Effusing long, indecent moans.

In Case You Are Forgetful

I am a thing without wings—
Grounded, flightless.
I am a bench away from conventional furniture,
A limb lobbed off to give view a better chance.

I am romance unchecked
And left to die in thin expletives—
Accusations, bitter bullets with preternatural aim,
Straight shots through unconscious refrain—
A singular defeat,
The martyrdoms of stolen life replete.

We see in taffeta casings
What we remove before completion.
The first stitch, a closing of an unresponsive wound.
The mourning, an afterthought
When the body is ruined.

Death (This is all just conjecture)

I Need to Keep Living Because

I've been trying to plot out my last words.
So far, I've come up with the impossibly succinct
And improbably overdone
"Ouch."

But it feels too "spur of the moment,"
And I don't want people thinking I didn't
agonize over this choice.

I tried rolling "I thought this was eternity"
Around my tongue a few times,
But it grew almost bovine,
A beefy muscle moving membranous minutia
around in flagrant finality.
So, no dice on that one either.

Maybe I'll say, "The curtain is finally drawn,"
Alluding to some secret sect of knowledge
Only my dying eyes can discern.

Maybe I'll accuse my therapist of murder
Or my dentist of philandering—
Maybe I'll make like a mother
And nurse my delusions back to life.

Crying, "He loves me, he loves me not.
Bring me my rose petals!"

Maybe I'll drone ad nauseam
About the different kinds of deaths
And compare mine to theirs—
"Didn't she look better in her drowning?"

What if I say, "God Bless Dictionaries,"
And I stutter and only get out the first syllable of
The last word and it ends up, "God Bless Dick,"
And Freud rolls over in his grave?

And my great grandmother rolls her eyes,
And everyone witness to my sorrowful passing is
rolling on the floor in hysterics.

What a way to go.
I need more time to think.

Death (This is all just conjecture)

It's Up in the Air

Today I am suicidal, passively so.
I have a tender consideration of things,
Like the soft slant of sunlight
Through variegated leaves.
I make my legs move to contrived rhythms,
Like death rattles and eulogies.
I eat mac and cheese on the barn porch for breakfast.
I think, *Who cares about fad diets*
Or the size of my grief?!
Both things will cycle out, eventually.
Today, I am suicidal.
Tomorrow, (maybe even tonight),
I will be euphoric again.
I suppose that's how it goes—
How meteoric.

Death and its Prerogative

It is a silent sentinel
Passively reaching—
Committed to that final hold,
Which alone,
Compels it.

Lust brings it low,
Touching the heels of swift feet and slow.
It has no need to rush over you—
It will come,
Indiscriminately,
In the end.

When it finds me,
I will greet it
With a knowing nod.

Until then—
I grate its head against my will
And tattoo its body on my calves.
So, it may laugh
to see its image
On fragile skin.

Death (This is all just conjecture)

Hometown and Tone, The Change of Song

The leaves are turning red-orange-gold
On the streets my hometown boasts.
The cats and cars look at me askance.
(I've forgotten the dress code for body and demeanor.)

The Baptist church has an old, old sign
That's supposed to read, "Bible preaching,"
But the "p" has fallen off—
And now, I guess they're reaching in biblical ways
To sway the world to their reality.

The days are slow and steady in my hometown green,
The sheen on hungry eyes too used to feeding—
Food for thought.
It eats you up inside.
The appetites of many leave you bleeding.

It is different in my home, in my hometown—
I am one inch higher on the wall.
The picture frames and pictures
Do not look like me at all.
They are red, raving lunatics
Whose smiles suggest suspicion
 Or suspension.

Some supplementary sin
To distract from the original.

It is different in my home, in my hometown—
My parents' knees are wearing down.
My father is one inch shorter on the wall.
The pictures do not look like him at all.

I see the memories
In the glass armoire,
But when I turn to greet them,
Sunbeams cloak them cold.
I am too old now
To feel free in my hometown—
The shadows house my childhood.
I feel the presence under tombstones,
Heavier now.

DEATH (THIS IS ALL JUST CONJECTURE)

Weakness In my Body

I have weakness in my body.
It is glory, the finality of frailty.
The promise of failure
In little lines along my mouth.
I am just south of twenty-four,
And I feel the world tear through me—
The days blur ...
And now my skin refuses to.
I am so grateful to be allowed to age,
But I'm afraid now.
I'm afraid.

Balance and Losing

My name is a curse on broken lips.
The syllables all scream at emptiness
That replicates my own.
I am nothing
And pull—
The very something,
Out of everything,
Until the void of me
Is full,
And I'm alone.

Death (This is all just conjecture)

Getting Older, On Needing

When I was younger,
I dreamed I was in a snowstorm so dense—
I had a rope around my middle,
Binding my cohort to my kidney, my liver.

I was not, however, tied—
I was cantilevered.
I heard the whisper of society
Come ghostly through white, bullet tears
That the sky leaked
Indefinitely.

There was nothing on the end of that rope.
(I was at mine.)
The world at hers—
We ached for otherness to attach ourselves to.

I was blank in her blankness,
Aware of the thankless—
Nature of nature when nurture ducks out.
I was small in a vastness that the
Vestige of thought could not touch.

There is no word
To save the soul
When the soul
Has no other hand—
To soothe it.

There is no brain that can smother
The touch of a brother,
The shoulder firm against shoulder,
When you get older
And find gravity in your breakfast toast
And your smile slips
Sentiment
To
Senility.

There, the long line,
The rope, flat against your palm,
Whose qualm is not with weather
But the fraying of your mind.

There, the short end,
The stick with splintered edges.
The hedges
Of your heart
That lets the lonely putter through—

Death (This is all just conjecture)

And you ...
In that dense, dark white—
The spite-less kiss of season
When reason falls to wayside.

You, alone, intone,
The echo of the epoch.
The empty that you feel
At the corner of your eye.
You, alone.
The rope so cantilevered
With frostbitten fingers,
Stuck straight out against
The barren spray.

ANIKA SNYDER

Things You Might Forget

In the felling of things—
Trees, laws,
The seventy-seven-year-old father
Slipped up on the stairs.
The baring of teeth at death and aging,
As if to stave off the gracelessness of their approach.
Memory, still febrile under living's touch,
Explodes out at the door frames,
The blowup mattress,
Anything it can catch in its fractious net.
"Remember this," the panic says.
"Remember the splayed-out father,
The slow fetid rot of breath, of tongue—
The dying in the once young face."
The destiny in the drowning,
A glimpse at further striving—
If luck allows.

Death (This is all just conjecture)

After the Ghost Leaves

After the ghost leaves, squeegee the ceiling.
Peel the cobwebs from the corners—
Foster concern for the cavernous nature of response.
What will you do with their absence?
Gloat?
Float?
Gently now—
The surface of your fear is sheer-faced and glacial.

A thumb tucked against a splitting hair,
A wordless transaction of the cavil calvary.
A dispensation, like a prayer
Above some final command,
To be loved, without doubting.
A figureless fight—
The ghost in the floorboards, the cupboards,
The thinnest of grins
Slung across tired old beams,
Like lights.

Prognosticate

The moths are dying in the dark.
They dart like panicked flies
Through tines
Of forked moonlight.

The moths hit tiny bodies against
Extinguished bulbs.
The cold reality of glass,
The last feeling the earth provides—
Nothing comforting in the wise
Unforgiving arms of fate.

I make matchbox coffins for the moths.
Only after, do I realize I've been cruel–
How can I let them rest on a substance
That could hold fire
But is bound
To being cool.

DEATH (THIS IS ALL JUST CONJECTURE)

VERISIMILITUDE

I feel my mortality thrum along my jawbone.

My metatarsals,

Aching from clenching, treading—

Down, hard.

Often softer feet fall behind,

Scoping for prints I emit.

We stand around the crowded in life,

Trying to escape the fawn's drawn body.

Taut tissues and tendons,

Trying at dying for the very first time.

"Breathe death out,"

We utter.

"Breathe life away,"

We coach.

She does not know how to die

Anymore than we do.

Guttural air seeps out through punctured lung—
Her tongue whets itself on living
For a moment more.
She tarries—
We cannot decide this for her.
We encourage, gently.
We try so hard not to offend.

Words spill, like envelope stamps
From my lips.
Deliver my sorrow to her dear deer form.
I quote Matthew Arnold
Because Lord knows—
My own edit on the edification of death
Would not suffice.

She is enlightened now, I suppose.
She knows
The world in its most intimate condition.
Her eyes are mirrors for the stars.
At night we see the constellation of their sight.

Death (This is all just conjecture)

Before We are Believed, We are Eradicated

Yesterday we lost the water tower.
It stood—
Perched atop a hill,
Like the gill
Of a particularly landbound fish,
The only water-based thing of industry—
For miles.

The last pieces of wood,
The penniless planks,
Plundered the favor of gravity
And gave into centrifugal force.
Collapsing,
As a soundless soliloquy—
The ardent architecture of amoral advice,
Something that sounds like giving
But means
Give up.

Yesterday we lost the water tower.
I did not see it fall.
Sometimes—
It is hard to believe in completeness
Because the end
Consumes us all.

ANIKA SNYDER

The Death of a Loved One

The walls will themselves apart—
A visible effort.
They, too, are near collapse.
I pat the walls.
They let me put my back against them—
We stay quiet for a while, breathing deep.

I am afraid to step away from the walls,
Afraid of gravity and my own diaphanous skin
That might tear in its parting
From illusionary stability.

My hands find throat,
Worry the hidden tube of esophagus.
Choke on brittle words—
Placeholders for meaning,
When meaning
Has no clothes to wear.

The walls will themselves apart
Because they know brokenness
And refuse to be so.
I do not know
How they do it.

Death (This is all just conjecture)

Two Ravens on a Line

Death and something questioning—
The long line, hunger in the very veins
You emptied just last week of blood.

Death on the power lines—
Two ravens rough hewn
In unkind renown.
The way the adverbs move through their beaks,
Almost alive, the verbose voices
Of the ones intended to quote,
"Nevermore"
Forever.

Death and something questioning—
A church emptied of its pastors.
The last hours
Should be spent in gilt instead of guilt.
I am built so incorrectly.
My soul has nowhere to fit.
So, I drop it at the doorstep
Of the local bar and try and find some way
To keep from going
Home.

Death (This is all just conjecture)

The Big J.C.

Jimmy Carter is dead.
When I was fifteen,
I went to his book signing
And toted the heavy,
Crumbling mess of my idolization
To the tip of the table
And laid it down with the small, blue book
He wrote just for me.

His eyes were little motes.
A boat—
Of indeterminable, structural status could float
Gently down, if encouraged.
Something so calm in the tide of them,
The trials and the choices,
Like currents overdone but pressing forward.

The line snaked
Through the maze of the bookstore.
I pressed my fingers against covers as I passed them.
I wandered
The halls
Of literacy
Like a liability.

Death (This is all just conjecture)

I choked on ambition,
Hoping to catch the drift
Of intellectual sadism,
As it beat the point to death.
But near that presidential presence,
I felt the piercing accuracy of poetic pause—
That something so small and fragile and human
Could have power
In such complete ways.

As I left that day,
The book,
Heavy now with a curling black signature,
Almost slipped out from under my arm,
To run itself to introspective grace—

May I bring it to his grave now?
I have a few more things to say.

Hopeful ending

I am feeling magnanimous. Here is the hopeful ending I will provide for the damage done by the patently unhopeful work preceding it.

Felt Tip

We have to tell me to slow down,
To keep up,
To talk slow,
Speak faster,
Listen up,
And butt out.

We have to tell me when we are joking
Because figurative speech
Makes my lymph nodes swell up.
(Don't you love a good reaction?)

We have to watch out for heavy stuff—
Because, no matter my dedication to strength training,
I am just not strong enough to handle it.

HOPEFUL ENDING

We have to keep close eyes on my body
Because it's cost me,
As it's cast me into risk after risk—
Without the knowledge of its folly.

We have to know the kind of pen I am,
So I can write my own narrative.
I offer up: felt tip
Because I felt the world tip into me—
And have not been alone
Since.

About the Author

Anika Snyder was born and raised in Northern California. She is a self-employed, self-proclaimed emotional mess who, at twenty-five, sought to publish the three-year-long mania-driven poetry that escaped her. With the help of loose social boundaries and an unquenchable desire to self-sabotage, she has extracted the emotional essence from her relationships and poorly functioning mental health in order to enlighten the world to the struggles of bipolar disorder ... and also to tell on herself.

Anika is a dropout of Sonoma State University and was once a patient featured in her childhood therapist's art therapy book. The poems found in this book offer insight, only insomuch as diagnostic criteria and the author hope beyond hope her psychiatrist will never read.

www.ingramcontent.com/pod-product-compliance
Lightning Source LLC
Chambersburg PA
CBHW050852160426
43194CB00011B/2130